Inhabiting the earth as a finite world

The research on which this book is based was carried out from 1973 to 1977 at the Academy of Architecture, Rotterdam, in collaboration with Erasmus University, Rotterdam.

Research group:
Willem van den Akker, Population, food, and the environment.
Piet Bennehey, Building problems in the Third World: test cases.
Richard Foqué, Project strategy and design methods.
Frits Mastenbroek, Civil engineering and budget analysis.
Jan van Middelkoop, Natural resources and energy.
Fred Muller, Editor; Design and coordination of simulation model.
Jan Trapman, Initiator; Project analysis and project coordination.

Third-year students at the National Higher Institute of Architecture and Town Planning, Antwerp, Belgium, took part in the project.

Inhabiting the earth as a finite world

An examination of the prospects of providing housing in a finite world in which prosperity is fairly shared, natural resources are not depleted, and the environment is protected.

Research group on living and surviving

Martinus Nijhoff Publishing
Boston/The Hague/London

With a preface by J. Gruijters,
Former Minister of Housing and Physical Planning

Library of Congress Cataloging in Publication Data

Research Group on Living and Surviving.
  Inhabiting the earth as a finite world.

  Bibliography: p.
  Includes index.
  1. Housing—Mathematical models. 2. Natural
resources—Mathematical models. I. Akker,
William van den. II. Muller, Fred. III. Title
HD7287.5.R45 1978   338.4'7'6908   78-13993
ISBN 0-0-89838-018-9

Distributors outside of North America:
Kluwer Academic Publishers Group
Distribution Centre
P.O. Box 322
3300 AH Dordrecht, The Netherlands

Translated by A. Cook, Ouddorp, the Netherlands
Original title: *Wonen met de wereld*

Preface

Since the 'sixties anxiety about the future of mankind has led to a number of major publications on the world's vital problems and the relationship between them, the best known being the reports to the Club of Rome.

This study of the problems of providing living accommodation for a rapidly growing world population, taking into account the limits that must be set to this growth, was started in 1973 at the Academy of Architecture and Erasmus University, Rotterdam, and testifies to the same anxiety. Inhabiting the Earth as a Finite World is the impressive result of a study of the consequences of meeting the just demand for good accommodation for all the earth's inhabitants, worked out with the aid of a world model and a number of case studies.

The value of models, especially very complex ones, is at present debatable. Nevertheless, they can often cast light on complex situations. The simplified form of the real situation, which every model in fact is, allows certain implications of decisions to be discerned and taken into account in planning. The comparison of the results of the study with the design process is a clear example of this.

It is interesting to note that the selection of materials and method of construction based on the results of the model leads not only to an economical, well-contrived design, but also makes for inclusion among the requirements aspects relevant to the situation, such as climate and socio-cultural backgrounds. The study gives some nice examples of this. When the conclusions are sometimes unexpected – for instance that based on the assumptions of Chapter 5, Surinam pile-dwellings are dearer per square metre than Dutch houses and that the amount of timber used is hardly justified if they are widely built – this encourages further critical reading.

As the group consisted largely of architects, housing design and comparison of design methods has received considerable attention. A group of students at the National Higher Institute of Architecture and Town Planning, Antwerp, made a major contribution on this subject.

The principles on which the group based its research nevertheless showed its awareness of the far wider underlying political implications of the problems. For one thing, most of the time they disregarded the possibility of new developments which might help to solve the dearth of natural resources. This is not only a useful justification of the study but is also indicative of a definite standpoint on the direction in which the group believed a solution ought to be sought. But its members have rightly pointed out the many uncertainties that demand great caution.

At 'Habitat', the United Nations conference on human settlements in Vancouver in 1976, an abridged version of this study was handed out to those present. There was a conviction then that its subject-matter and method would provide valuable information for many people, and this definitive publication, too, is worthy of the attention of a wide audience.

J. Gruijters
Former Minister of Housing and Physical Planning

Contents

Introduction

In the midst of a widespread belief in progress the warning signs of the dangers threatening mankind were hardly noticed. People expectantly followed the growth in medical knowledge. They happily noted the progress in curing hitherto incurable diseases, the decrease in infant mortality, and the rise in the average expectation of life. In the midst of ever newer scientific and technological advances we have grown up with a belief in an unbounded future. Many human beings live in the dream that they are the chief occupants of the earth, perhaps even the lords of the universe. With the stars within our reach it seemed pointless to husband the wealth of materials and resources around us. This was the atmosphere in which many people came to think and act in terms of growth.

In our rude awakening from this dream, however, we find ourselves in a very tenuous film of air, land, and water on which life depends. In the interplay of all the vital processes that prevail in this, mankind is poised in a very vulnerable system which can easily be thrown out of equilibrium.

At first there were only isolated signals warning against the increase in population, the extinction of plants and animals, and the widening gap between rich and poor. Later the interrelationship between these symptoms started to become clear. When combined together, the individual problems proved more alarming than had been suspected. People came to the conclusion that this course of events was leading to total disaster and that existing trends would inexorably annihilate our system of life.

Hence all these problems can be brought nearer to solution only if they are studied as related problems. Any improvement can only be made on this basis.

These conclusions have led on all sides to an upsurge in thinking about the causes of these developments and the action that ought to be taken to turn the tide. At a world level the United Nations has organised a number of conferences on specific problems such as pollution of the environment, the population problem, food supply. These conferences ended by making recommendations for action.

Besides this, international study groups were briefed to examine various aspects of the problems in greater detail. And political parties also started taking action. Proposals for material and social changes have meanwhile been incorporated in many party programmes.

Many people become terrified and uncertain in the midst of this flood of information and recommendations. Most have hardly been able to benefit yet from the tremendous advances in technology. Indeed, they have mostly only been allowed to pluck its sour fruits. Yet they had hoped that these golden possibilities would sometime become reality for them as well. And they have quite rightly been astounded when those who have in fact had the benefit of all the progress now proclaim that growth must stop and prosperity be limited. Most of the underprivileged still live in such conditions that this information does not even reach them, and they are hit harder still when they face its consequences. Most of the wealthy, who do know, strongly resist any sweeping changes because they fear their effects. Anxiety springs up about the distribution of prosperity: what will be left? Anxiety, too, about reducing the consumption of energy and raw materials, because prosperity depends on them. There is a vague realisation of common responsibility for the exploitation of our fellow men and natural resources. But the problems are too vast and too unspecified to determine the individual's personal responsibility.

Nor is it clear what all this means to one's personal position. One major reason is that recommendations are mostly couched in vague terms: 'Freedom, equality, and suitable living conditions for all'; or, 'The earth's non-renewable resources should be used in such a way as to guard against the danger of their future exhaustion, and to ensure that the advantages of such use will benefit the whole world' (U.N. Conference, Stockholm, see Melgert and Mok, 1973).

There is still no clear picture of the possible consequences for the individual and for the world that comes after us. And yet this is of the utmost importance. The necessary political measures cannot be taken unless the population is ready to help to put them into effect. First of all, this means that anxiety and uncertainty must be removed wherever possible. *It must become clear what will happen if we do indeed inhabit the earth as a finite world and not at its expense.* What would happen if we consistently complied with all the recommendations? What would the world be like? In particular: what would our immediate habitat be like?

These problems were also raised at the U.N. Conference on human settlements in Vancouver in June 1976. An important feature was a resolution on national control of people's own territory and the rights of population groups to national territories (the Palestinians). Many problems were delegated to an organisation that would be newly formed. At the conference of non-government organisations (the Forum) there was more differentiated treatment of the problems. Only a few examples can be mentioned:

- The uncontrolled growth of conurbations through so many people leaving agricultural areas. The problem of the millions fleeing from the poverty-ridden countryside can be solved only by rural redevelopment. The amounts at present being spent on urban development should be devoted to harmonious development of the country as a whole.
- There is no point in considering housing problems in isolation and thinking out solutions for them. The only possibility of success is an integrated approach to the problems of employment, food supply, housing, medical and social care, education, and development.
- The authorities simply cannot solve *all* the problems themselves. They must provide scope for people to seek their own solutions.
- There is growing resistance to land speculation.
- Much attention was paid to energy and environmental problems. In this context, a recommendation was formulated to stop further development of nuclear power stations and to use every means of seeking alternative energy sources.
- It has become clear that the entire problem of human settlements is a political problem far more than a technical one.

In 1973 the authors began to wonder whether it would be possible to solve a number of these problems – not necessarily in precise terms, but in about the right dimensions. Initial enquiries indicated enough possibilities of bringing at least some of these questions closer to an answer. The principal problems and recommendations could be listed and some of their implications worked out in greater detail.

A world computer model is needed to link these data together quantitatively. We proposed to set up this model so that the results would show that share of the natural resources to which every human being would be entitled, how much energy he would be able to use, and what proportion of the prosperity would be his due under these conditions.

As it is impossible in such a project to clarify all the aspects involved in inhabiting the earth as a finite world, some limitation was necessary. The study is focused on designing homes for people to live in: the individual habitat and the individual home in a finite world. It was decided to set up the computer model so that the results would provide enough data for a basis for designing living accommodation.

The net result was that a research project called 'Inhabiting the Earth as a Finite World' was launched at the Academy of Architecture, Rotterdam.

The first results were presented at the U.N. Conference on human settlements in Vancouver (F. Muller, J. Trapman, R. Foqué, 1976). The book you now have has been written by the research group on *living and surviving*. Its members trust that reading it will be as surprising an experience as was the work on the project itself.

1. The dangers threatening mankind

From his very beginning the outside world has threatened man's existence. Lacking the natural protection of fur, having no great strength or claws, with poor eyesight, a poor runner, climber, and swimmer, and unable to fly, he has had to answer the challenges of nature by using his brains. Acquisition and transfer of wisdom and knowledge, and making and using tools, are his most important means of defence. His need to respond to all the challenges was described by Toynbee as one of the most important incentives to human development. But particularly in recent years man himself is proving to be the greatest threat to the survival of his own species. This is reflected in its most extreme form in the technical and military apparatus he has built up. Sparing neither cost nor effort, he has succeeded in building the means of wiping out the human race, himself included. A solution to this problem is being sought through international talks. The study embodies a number of measures which may diminish the causes of conflict situations, such as better income distribution.

Quite apart from the threat of war, there are many other potentially disastrous developments, such as the population explosion, the food problem, pollution, and the depletion of scarce resources.

1.1 The interrelation of the problems

Individual aspects of these problems have been searchingly studied for some time. It was in the 'sixties that the System Dynamics Group of the Massachusets Institute of Technology (M.I.T.), led by J. Forrester, made the first attempt to study the world's essential problems in their mutual relationship. Their method originated from the theory of complex systems. These systems in fact prove to consist of the interplay of many chains of comparatively simple feedback loops.

An international group of individuals, including several major industrialists, decided to take action out of concern about the course of events. In 1970 the Club of Rome which they formed requested D. L. Meadows, to-

gether with an interdisciplinary team of scientists, to study the interrelationship of a number of world-embracing problems. The point of departure was
the present social and economic structures, and existing trends were extrapo-
lated. The conclusion was that the consequences of continuing present trends
would be disastrous. One of the principal causes is that practically all variables in their study, such as population, material and energy consumption,
and pollution, are characterised by exponential growth. In the last analysis,
exponential growth is incompatible with stable equilibrium.

Exponential growth occurs when a quantity increases by a constant percentage, known as the growth rate. There is a simple correlation between
growth rate and doubling time: with a growth rate of 0.1 percent a year
the doubling time is about 700 years; at 1 percent it is 70 years, and so on.

Exponential growth is a common occurrence. Bacteria and other microor-
ganisms multiply exponentially until a catastrophe hits them through lack of
food, lack of space, or a pile-up of metabolic products. Among higher plants
and animals there are plagues of weeds, rats, and so on. The water-weed
Elodea canadensis in Leiden in the previous century; *Senecio congestus*, a bog-
plant rampant in the drained South Flevo polder; mosquitoes when the
Zuider Zee was closed off; starlings in North America; and rabbits in
Australia are all well-known examples of population explosions caused by
exceptional conditions such as the absence of natural enemies.

The population is also subject to exponential growth. In 1650 there were
only 500 million people in the whole world; the growth rate was 0.3 percent
per annum with a doubling time of 230 years. By 1970 the world population
had already reached 3.6 billion with a growth rate of 2.1 percent and a doubling time of only 33 years. This illustrates how serious the problem is.

Lastly, natural resources are also being consumed exponentially. Take
aluminium, the consumption of which is increasing at the rate of 6.4 percent
per annum (doubling consumption in 11.1 years), copper 4.6 percent (doubling time 15.4 years), iron 1.8 percent (38.9 years), natural gas 4.7 percent
(14.9 years), and petroleum 3.9 percent (18.1 years).

In the early stages of exponential growth no one worries much because its
extent is still so slight. This may explain why the human race has become
aware of the dangers so late in the day. It is at the last moment that the process
becomes so fast and tremendous changes take place. Then there is little time
left to turn the tide. Delays of only a few years in redirecting the tendencies
that cause exponential growth may be a matter of life and death for millions of
people.

Publication of the first Report of the Club of Rome had a traumatic effect.

The alarming conclusions of the investigations received the fullest attention throughout the world and mobilised public opinion. But there was also serious criticism on many sides. This concerns both the relationships between the various elements of the model and also the lack of certain important factors. For instance, the Report pays little attention to the influence of social factors. There is also much criticism because the causes of exponential growth are not analysed, especially regarding the role of big industrial organisations and the power they wield. Despite all this criticism of parts of the study, there are many who believe that the principal conclusions regarding the disastrous consequences of exponential growth are true on the whole.

In many cases the criticism has brought new viewpoints, and increased attention is being paid to the problems. F. Muller (1973), for instance, examined the possibilities of obtaining more acceptable results with the aid of economic and political measures. At the end of 1974 the second Report to the Club of Rome appeared: *Mankind at the turning point* (M. Mesarovic and E. Pestel, 1974). This study no longer takes the world as a whole but divides it into 10 regions. Its results largely substantiate the conclusions of the first Report. To solve the problems, it recommends a complex of growth-controlling measures, which it calls 'organic growth'. Some of the large-scale technological solutions the authors suggest, however, would seem to clash with the small-scale ecosystems they want to sustain.

Other groups' aim is complete stability: zero growth, as they put it. The problems connected with this are analysed by A. Sauvy (1973) for instance. He rejects absolute zero growth but nevertheless thinks that moderate yet sufficiently shattering events should bring mankind to its senses.

In Britain in 1972, *Blueprint for survival* was published. It puts special emphasis on social structures and the impending destruction of ecosystems.

All these studies again confirm that the problems can only be solved in context. But this context is so complex that parts of it have to be studied separately. These parts are gone into individually in the following sections.

1.2 Natural resources

Exponential growth is the reason why many materials are likely to be depleted before long. New reserves will of course be discovered as time goes by. Better methods are also becoming available for recovering materials which are as yet unworkable. As the earth hardly produces any more of these materials, or none at all, reserves are in any case finite. If the exponential increase in consumption continues, a doubling or even a tenfold increase in reserves will only help us a little. The cost of recovery is constantly increasing, because the most accessible reserves are exploited first. More and more energy and equipment is needed, which again speeds up the process of depletion.

Even materials that are produced each year, such as food and timber, have become scarce. There are big food shortages. There has been large-scale deforestation. Over-fishing is even threatening to make certain kinds of fish extinct.

Chapter 3 will discuss the raw materials situation in detail.

1.3 The food problem

In 1974 the United Nations organised a World Food Conference in Rome. This, too, disclosed that the food shortage was not an isolated problem. The problems are so interwoven with economic and social structures that only fundamental changes can solve them. The readiness of the rich nations in this direction certainly was not such as to shake Rome to its foundations. Proposals for setting up food depots to fight hunger in the world are little more than repressing the symptoms. The situation is patently alarming: the world food organisation, F.A.O., calculated in 1974 that 500 million people were on the verge of death from starvation.

Food production depends on the area of suitable land and the methods of making it productive. An investigation by H. Linneman (1976) estimated possible food production in the year 2010 at approximately 2.5 times the present annual production. For this, however, structural improvements were essential.

Summing up the various studies of this subject gives us the following findings:

1. it is wrong to produce food in only a number of places, to store it, and then sell it to the poor. It should be grown wherever possible at the place it is needed, which would also save energy and transport. Storage of food reserves should be as decentralised as possible;
2. at present 86 percent of all artificial fertiliser is used in the rich countries. This is not compatible with the proper management of materials, energy, and the environment;
3. the use of pesticides should be limited.

1.4 The population problem

In discussing exponential growth, we gave some figures on the increase in population. The world population is at present growing at the rate of 2.1 percent per annum. But this is the average. Growth varies from 0.5 percent in some European countries (with a doubling time of 140 years) to over 3 percent in many countries in South America, Africa, and Asia (with a doubling time of less than 25 years).

The huge population increase is due primarily to a fall in the death rate. In the Western countries infant mortality has dropped to 1.5 percent, and the medical profession looks on even this as a challenge. We soon forget that barely two centuries ago fewer than half the people reached adulthood in these selfsame countries. It has long been realised that this trend could have most perilous consequences. As far back as 1798 Malthus warned against over-population.

Even on the assumption that an optimal birth-control system will be adopted world wide before long, the conclusion is startling. All research indicates that even then it would take over 40 years for population growth to come to a standstill. The main reason is that most of the year 2000's parents have already been born. Even with good birth control the present world population would still roughly double. By the year 2020, therefore, we shall have to allow for a world population of at least 7 billion.

This great population growth brings a number of problems. Many non-industrialised countries have a very uneven age structure. The population explosion has led to a situation in which nearly half the inhabitants are younger than 15 years. This can obviously cause serious economic and social problems.

Furthermore, crowding occurs where populations are densely concentrated. Although much sociological research is carried out into the consequences of too many people living close together, it is not yet possible to indicate what 'too many' means in this context. But it is clear that excessive concentrations must be avoided. This also means that special attention must be paid to the habitat in which man will not only have to sustain himself as an individual but in which he must also be able to develop.

Internationally, too, the population problem has received great attention. In Bucharest in 1974 the United Nations held a conference on this problem. The poor countries put great emphasis on the connection between population growth and prosperity. Population growth can be stopped only if the general standard of living is raised. And it is the rich countries that can do much to raise it if they so wish.

1.5 The effects on the environment

Man has made drastic changes on the earth which imperil the environment.
Rachel Carson (1963) sounded the first alarm. She pointed out that pesticides
used in vast quantities against diseases and insects can have harmful, worldwide effects. These chemicals contain poisons which can hardly be broken
down naturally and spread throughout the environment. In particular, she
attacked persistent chlorinated hydrocarbons such as DDT, which are stored
in animal tissues and reach the natural cycle via food chains.

Modern farming methods make intensive use of artificial fertilisers. The
annual consumption is about 10 million tonnes. They have a number of
drawbacks. Apart from the fact that fertiliser production requires large
amounts of fossil fuels, a big proportion is washed away unused, by rain and
irrigation. The natural equilibrium is seriously disturbed by the overabun-
dant growth of algae this causes. Consequently, not only fish but numerous
other organisms die off and the water loses its assimilative capacity.

In the long run, fertilisers are not the answer to the food problem. Beyond a
certain limit excessive amounts have to be used to obtain only a small increase
in production. Lastly, fertilisers cannot stop the soil being exhausted.

Society produces a vast amount of waste. It had long been thought that the
earth's self-regulating system would neutralise this. But these possibilities
have long been exhausted. Waste has become an immediate threat to life on
earth.

Heavy metals such as mercury, lead, arsenic, chromium, and nickel are very
dangerous; the same applies to oil discharged straight into the sea, and hydrocarbons precipitated from the atmosphere. Then there are radioactive
wastes such as iodine 131, xenon 153, strontium 90, and caesium 137.

Thermal pollution of rivers by cooling water is also very dangerous. The
biological equilibrium of rivers and lakes is seriously disturbed by an increase
in temperature of only a few degrees. There is hardly any chance of living
organisms surviving in water warmer than 34° C.

Besides pollution of soil and water, the air is also being badly affected. In
1967 approximately 13.4 billion tonnes of CO_2 were released by fossil fuel
combustion. This carries a tremendous amount of heat into the atmosphere.
The effects this has on the climate are almost incalculable. There is a widespread fear that it can have disastrous consequences, and the same applies to
supersonic jet aircraft exhaust gases and freon aerosol propellant.

It is, of course, much simpler to take action nationally rather than worldwide. Many countries took measures against pollution in the 'sixties.

Examples are the series of acts: the Water Quality Act (1965), the Air Quality Act (1967), and the Solid Waste Disposal Act (1965) in the United States. Some spectacular local successes have been the return of life and fish to the North American lakes, the restoration of the environment in the Baikal Lake in the U.S.S.R., and the return of fish to the River Thames near London.

Very many countries have started monitoring pollution by industrial processes, the use of pesticides is being restricted, and the use of chemicals critically examined. After political parties included environmental care in their election programmes, special ministries of the environment were set up.

The misgivings are also noticeable in physical planning. Development and regional plans are taking more notice of environmental aspects. Efforts are being made to spread industry, suppress traffic, provide green belts, and so on. Small-scale developments are being given more and more preference.

As to the lines along which a solution might be sought, the situation in China is interesting. Although not intended as such, the People's Republic of China can be looked upon as an experimental situation for solving a number of fundamental problems. Despite criticism of the excessive use of pesticides and the encroachment, in Western eyes, upon the freedom of the individual, the country nevertheless provides examples of possible future development.

In Europe, after years of laborious negotiations, basic agreement was reached in 1976 on limiting the discharge of chemical waste into the River Rhine. This agreement should become operational in 1978. But as yet there is no agreement on other types of pollution, such as the discharge of salt and heat.

A major incentive to international consultation was the conference on the environment in Stockholm in 1972. It resulted in a plan of action with recommendations for a better environment and new U.N. machinery for coordinating action against environmental problems. A declaration was adopted urging freedom, equality, and suitable living conditions for all. Lastly, the wish was expressed that the depletion of scarce raw materials should be prevented and that their use should benefit the whole of mankind.

1.6 The significance of technological developments

One of the many people emphasising the need to consider all the elements of integrated systems is Peters (1973). He comes to the following conclusion:

The iron law of nature of increasing entropy is the most universal way of materially explaining the law of the conservation of misery. According to this law, the ultimate solution of present world problems cannot be expected from technology. It is not only a question of doing certain things, but also of not doing certain things, both individually and collectively.

A classic example of inadvertent changes in the ecological system is the construction of the Aswan Dam on the River Nile. The lake that was formed provides a substantial part of Egypt's electricity and makes it possible to irrigate a large agricultural area. The fertile mud from the Nile, however, settled in the still waters of the lake, and the irrigated soil became fertile. A parasite, the Bilharzia, developed in the slow-moving waters and caused a major epidemic. Worse still, the flourishing fishing industry off the coast was largely ruined, because the fish no longer found enough food in the poorer river water flowing into the sea. The modern methods and the results of medical science which penetrated to the people (though without any form of social guidance) through the construction of the dam greatly improved their health. During the dam's construction the population thus increased to such an extent that even the new arable land was not able to feed them.

The products of technology will have to be looked at in a different light. Their efficiency is still far from perfect. Take the automobile: on average, it requires 23,000 kWh to build. Using it to drive 20,000 km consumes another 23,000 kWh. Illich (1973) calculated how long a man has to work in order to drive a car. Converted to Dutch standards, a person driving 15,000 km expends on depreciation, maintenance, oil and petrol, plus the time he spends in the car, as much as he earns in 916 hours. He therefore travels at the rate of 16 km per hour's work. And this does not include the construction of roads, hospitalisation, and so on.

Technological developments are indispensable for seeking substitutes for scarce resources. Research into this is only making slow progress, because motivation is a matter of short-term costs, prices, and profits. Research regarding alternative energy sources is dealt with in Chapter 3.

1.7 Distribution of prosperity

The conviction that every human being, irrespective of race, creed, or sex, is fundamentally the same is gaining more and more ground. Ethical motives supported by ethnological research have contributed much to this conviction. The realisation that domination of one human being by another is no longer acceptable was one factor that sparked off the process of decolonisation. By extension, economic inequality is becoming less and less acceptable as well.

So far, world development has led to vast differences between rich and poor. But it has meanwhile become evident that world systems are so interwoven that there will no longer be any possibility of localised avoidance of general trends. The gaps between the various groups are widening quickly. If a world catastrophe is to be avoided, a common effort will be needed; this has to be one world or none.

The poor have become aware of their poverty, and of their power. They are rightly demanding a fair share of overall prosperity. In February 1975 the 104 delegates to the conference of Third World Nations at Algiers demanded a radical reform of the world economy, aiming at a fourfold increase in the poor nations' share of world prosperity in the next twenty five years. They pointed out that the nations present at the conference represented 70 percent of the world population but had only 7 percent of the income.

More and more people in many countries are becoming convinced that incomes are not fairly shared. Social and political organisations are pressing for the equitable distribution of incomes. In the Netherlands the government in its Interim Paper on Incomes Policy (1975) said: "Fair distribution means that only income differentials which compensate for differences in effort should exist." By means of scientific research, efforts are being made to arrive at a theory of equitable income distribution which would be acceptable for the vast majority of the population. Tinbergen (1975) proposes describing as equitable a situation in which prosperity is the same for all; he regards the utility function as the same for everyone. With certain assumptions, *equitable* income distribution then corresponds to *equal* income distribution, although this is not *necessarily* so. Nevertheless, our first objective will be an income distribution in which there will be no difference in income between rich and poor nations.

Differences in national prosperity are still very great. The per capita income in the United States in 1970 was nearly $ 5,000 and in most European countries nearly $ 3,000, while many African and Asian countries had no more than $ 100. The relationships these figures disclose flow from existing economic structures. The explanatory memorandum to the Dutch Foreign Ministry's estimates as early as 1973 said:

The ending of colonial relationships has not put an end to the exercise of power by the rich nations over the poor nations. By means of a dominant position in international trade and capital transactions and the control of science and technology, the rich nations can continue their position at the centre and skim off prosperity. This process is often described as exploitation.

Similar mechanisms governed relations between rich and poor countries many centuries ago. But what is new is that more people have become aware of them and want to put an end to them. The sixth special session of the United Nations General Assembly in April/May 1974 adopted two resolutions calling for the establishment of a new international order. Such a new world order will not only have to determine the nations' acts but especially those of the multinationals. These problems are meanwhile being examined by a number of study groups participating in the RIO Project (Reshaping the International Order, Tinbergen, 1976).

On the basis of the recommendations made at international level, let us now formulate the principles for research aimed at putting these recommendations into practice.

Principles of the study

This chapter catalogues the difficulties liable to occur in society in the near future and the measures recommended for dealing with them. The purpose of the project is to study the implications of these recommendations as regards living accommodation, adopting the following principles:

1. *The problems can ultimately be solved only by worldwide international con-sultation. The study assumes that the necessary organisations will be set up and that the necessary measures will be carried out.*
2. *Despite the utmost efforts with regard to birth control, linked with structural improvements, we must allow for a world population of at least 7 billion by 2020.*
3. *The use of scarce raw materials will have to be limited to prevent their being exhausted and to obtain enough time to develop adequate alternatives.*
4. *Prosperity must be equitably shared.*
5. *Adequate measures will have to be built in to keep pollution within such limits that the environment can be preserved.*
6. *We will not count on new developments solving the problem of raw material shortages but adopt the principle of present-day technologies including exist-ing possibilities of substitution and recycling.*
7. *Living accommodation for the year 2020 will have to be designed within precisely specified limits.*

These principles obviously have direct political implications. The political strategies that may follow from them are not discussed explicitly in this study.

One consideration is that it is better for the results first to be the subject of discussion, whence an answer may be found to the question of the desirability of such a world. We cannot start too early with this. The longer we take, the more likely we are to have no choice, while the very question of its desirability or not may no longer apply. In any case, the results of this study must not be looked upon as utopian ideals but as building bricks for the development of political strategies.

2. Systems approach as a research method

2.1 Research strategy

Chapter 1 has made it clear that the objective should be a society which does not exhaust its limited resources and allows everyone to benefit from them.

The object of our study was to visualise what the results of this could be. Because of limited time, manpower, and financial resources, it was impossible to do this for all aspects of human life. The study had to be limited to man and his habitat. An effort was therefore made to gain an idea of the consequences on living accommodation of diverting and stopping exponential growth. The fact that most of the members of the research group are architects did, of course, play an important role in the choice of this subject. This entailed the risk of a one-sided, architectural approach. But the contribution from the economic sciences provided by one of the members, together with the expert advice obtained on other subjects, had a corrective effect and gave the study an interdisciplinary character.

Understanding of the method employed may help the reader to penetrate to the essentials of the results. Besides the language of figures and statistics, which may seem abstract and absolute, an attempt was made to give shape to several specific housing units which could still be built within the general principles. An effort has been made, based on the discipline of the architect, to depict housing within the limits imposed on growth. Perhaps limitation to the habitat will enable the reader to recognise himself and assess his possibilities. In areas other than living accommodation the study also produced surprising results and conclusions.

There are four distinct stages in the ultimate research strategy: the problems and the principles, the exploratory stage, development of the simulation model, and the design stage. These are illustrated in Figure 2.1.

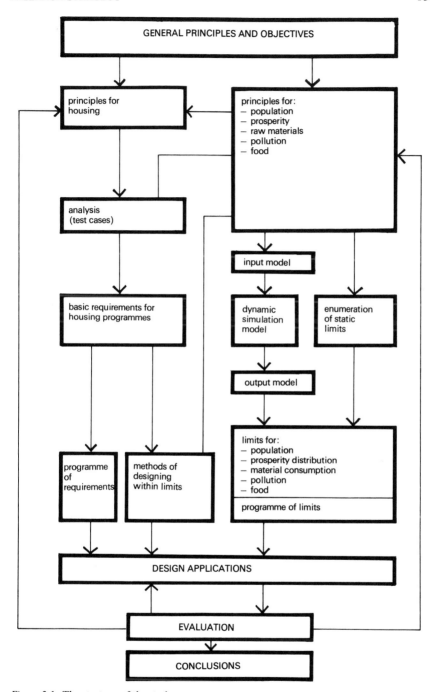

Figure 2.1. The strategy of the study.

2.1.1 Problems and principles

At this stage the initial problems are delved into and the principles and objectives defined.

This has been based on an extensive study of literature, much research, talks with experts, and team discussions. This gave a deeper understanding of the problems of exponential growth and the crises this causes. On this basis the principles were formulated as in Chapter 1. At this stage it was also decided which methods would be used in the study: i.e. the systems approach, the use of models, various methods of analysis, and the processing of statistical material.

2.1.2 Exploratory stage

Initial formulation of the objectives is the basis for the exploratory stage. The project strategy is now split into two parallel lines of research:

1. Research into the possibilities of a world simulation model for living accommodation based on quantitative parameters such as materials, energy, manhours, and money. From here on this model occupies a key position in the study. It had to be examined whether it was possible to analyse habitations on the basis of the above parameters. In order to obtain some diversity, three test cases are analysed in Chapter 5: a pile-dwelling in the Caribbean, a dwelling developed for Ghana by the U.N., and a largely prefabricated house in the Netherlands.
2. In order to gather more knowledge on which to base a specification of requirements research was carried out into the qualitative aspects of the accommodation process. Although these are not gone into here, they were the basis for the individual designs in Chapter 8, in which the results fully emerge.

2.1.3 The model stage

The results of the preceding stage made us more convinced than ever that a model approach to the process of accommodation is possible in terms of energy, materials, labour, and cost. Pursuing this, therefore, a design method must be developed by which accommodation can be designed with reference to quantitative criteria. In view of the principles applied. it is important to know the limits within which these parameters can vary, if prosperity is shared equitably.

Requirements which the simulation model and design method should satisfy are:

1. The model must furnish information on the permissible limits for energy and raw material consumption, the permissible quantity and maximum cost of accommodation. The principal factors are population growth, depletion of raw materials, pollution of the environment, income distribution, and the economic life of the accommodation. These concepts will be gone into further in Chapters 3 and 4, while the structure of the model will be described in detail in Chapter 6. Any model adopts a number of assumptions. Wherever an assumption had to be made this has been explicitly stated, if possible with the arguments on which the choice was based. Other parameters can, of course, be incorporated in the model as well. The output of the model gives a specification of limits with which future housing units should comply.

2. The development of a systematic design method must enable the designer to build following the specification of limits from the initial stage of the design process. This method is based on a system-orientated approach enabling designed forms of accommodation to be checked against the quantitative limits. An important feature in this respect is the development of an evaluation model which can quickly check any design against the specification of limits and in this way provide a permanent feedback. The method is explained in greater detail in Chapter 7, while Appendix C gives an example of a complete evaluation.

2.1.4 Design stage

The feasibility of the designed accommodation and the basic assumptions and hypotheses can be verified with reference to the model and the specifications developed in the preceding stage.

An initial series of trial designs were made by 20 third-year students at the National Higher Institute of Architecture and Town Planning, Antwerp. These outside designers constituted a check on the feasibility of the proposed design methods. The principal results are summarised in Chapter 7.

After these designs had been evaluated, the model and specifications could be adjusted further. This led to a set of usable requirements for the designer. They were tested by several members of the team themselves; the results are discussed in Chapter 8. These designs are intended as examples of practical possibilities. The socio-cultural and political backgrounds relate to a general underlying philosophy of living in a world in which values and standards have a very different meaning.

2.2 The model approach

In this study the systems-theory approach occupies an important place. Systems theory provides an adequate set of instruments for studying complex problem situations. One of the methods is that of structuring. To approach complexity in an orderly pattern makes it more comprehensible, and it can be discussed and manipulated. This is known as the dimensioning of complexity.

The model concept occupies a key position in this process. Models are invariably based on an analogy in the sense of Wieser (1959), i.e. an illustration of the same function in various materials based on various principles. The essential feature of an analogy between certain systems is that they function in the same way and hence have the same basic mechanisms.

A model describes the interaction between various elements and, to a lesser extent, the elements themselves. In this context Bertels and Nauta (1969) define a model in its historical perspective: 'A model is a concrete representation of situations and entities in nature and history in a collection of symbols.'

A more abstract definition of greater value for the present study is that of Apostel (1960): 'If one uses a known system B independent of system A to obtain information about A by means of B, then B is a model of A.'

Clearly, a model is never identical to the system which it depicts. Maturana, McCulloch, and Pitts (1959) state the essential condition that models can only depict clearly defined functions. A full description and full understanding of the functions is also needed before they can be put into a model. This leads to Wieser's hypothesis (1959) that highly complex systems cannot be embraced completely by a model. There is always a residue not capable of rational description. Wieser's starting-point is a biological system, the problem being how to embody it in a technical system without loss of complexity. In the case of a machine there is always a rationally thought-out plan where irrational factors can only creep in when it is put into effect; but in systems in which man also appears as an element, the plan itself is already full of irrational elements.

Yet the use of models whose principles are not clearly and exhaustively defined, has clearly proved their value, especially in the social sciences (see, for instance, Buckley, 1967). Their use is based on heuristic techniques: methods for finding a general, exploratory way through very complex situations.

The uncertainty content is therefore fairly large. In demarcating complexity, the models provide knowledge and information about the actual situation. Further, two important questions can be asked about models:
1. Is a model comparable with a scientific hypothesis?
2. Can a model have the value of a scientific theory?

These are questions about the conclusive force of a model and its general validity. Beer (1966) deals with this in great detail and answers both questions in the negative.

In our opinion, however, it must be possible to formulate hypotheses regarding the functioning of certain processes with the aid of a model. It is true that a model has no conclusive force itself, but comparison with the actual system which the model depicts always permits the model to be rejected if its results disagree with reality.

This viewpoint assumes every model to be a specific way of representing a system, with the object of gaining more knowledge of how the system operates. Another important facet regarded by Foqué (1975, 1976) as fundamental to critical employment of the model concept is the model's own structural laws. A model is always a description of an aspect of reality. A reduction in experience is, of course, inherent in every description, a reduction to forms that can be described with symbols. But this would be hazardous only if using the model were to be presented as the only correct approach.

In order to know the principles of a method, the underlying axioms must also be examined. A model approach has its own postulates and its own limitations which influence the result. In this sense the use of models is not purely and simply a problem of reduction but also one of transforming reality into a model. From this aspect, therefore, it is of the utmost importance in this study to indicate clearly the points of departure and the basic mechanisms of the model and to check the results against these.

Conclusions and principles for a model

As with any statistical material the figures we use do not claim to be completely accurate. The data on which a model is based and the relationships used in it often include a wide safety margin. Although the results of a model are stated in exact figures, we should realise that these must be looked upon as approximations.

3. Seeking general data for a dynamic world-model

3.1 Population

According to the United States Bureau of the Census, the world population on 28 March, 1976 had reached 4 billion people. It took only sixteen years to add the fourth billion, and the next billion will probably take only thirteen years.

The decline in infant mortality and the advances in science have brought about a constant reduction in the death rate. As the birth rate has not fallen as quickly, the rate of population growth has steadily increased. This is, in fact, a case of super-exponential growth. The present mean growth rate is 2.1 percent per annum.

There are some 328,000 births every day compared with 133,000 deaths, so the world population is increasing by 195,000 a day. The Museum of Science and Industry in Chicago has an enormous panel showing the situation from moment to moment: the world population is increasing at the rate of one person every 2.25 seconds.

This book has already pointed out that the overwhelming growth of the world population constitutes one of the principal threats to a stable world system.

This growth can be halted with birth control. But there is little international agreement on what action to take. This lack of unanimity has its origins partly in socio-economic and ethico-religious backgrounds. Countries with a severe shortage of labour even encourage population growth. In the German Democratic Republic propaganda is made for building large families, and the same applies in the Soviet Union.

Many South American countries are also trying to increase the birth rate for a variety of reasons. In Brazil one reason for this policy is the government's attempt to populate the country's extensive interior. But attention may also be drawn to the great influence which the Roman Catholic Church, with its opposition to birth control, still has in these countries.

The rejection of any form of birth control by Islamic leaders led to Saudi Arabia not attending the Bucharest Population Conference in 1974.

In countries where social security is inadequate a family of children is often a sheer necessity for survival. Only recently, Madame Suharto, the Indonesian President's wife and the mother of twelve children, said that most Indonesians wanted a lot of children to ensure that they would be cared for in their old age. Nevertheless, the Indonesian government is making every effort to control the population explosion, like many other Asian countries.

Conclusions and basic assumptions for a model

Though opinions on the number of people the earth could feed and accommodate vary greatly, the present super-exponential growth will obviously have disastrous consequences. Most people are convinced that the population will have to be stabilised in order to avoid this. But research has shown:

1. *that stabilisation cannot be achieved less than 40 years after constant fertility has been achieved;*
2. *that by then the population will be twice as great as at the start of that period. These findings will also have to be taken into account in the present model. Moreover, the process of stabilisation has got under way in the rich countries earlier than in the poor ones, and stabilising action will have a delayed effect in the poor countries. The objective will be a stabilised population by the year 2020.*

Here we should like to point out some relevant social developments which the expected increase in the population might bring about. A great deal of knowledge, understanding, and organisation will be needed to prevent the vast number of people doing too much harm to the natural environment. In addition to all the measures to protect this, considerable attention will have to be paid to the conurbations in which people have to live and work. With a population twice the size, the present trend towards unbridled urbanisation will certainly call for totally new ideas and action, in order to avoid endless urban areas. The need to arrange such areas so that every individual occupies a place which suits him will probably become very pressing.

3.2 Food

3.2.1 The starving world

Of all the dangers threatening mankind the rapidly increasing food shortage is the most alarming. Millions of people die of starvation every year. In India and Pakistan 140 out of every 1,000 babies die before their first birthday; in Zambia as many as 260. In most cases the recorded cause of death is some disease or other. It is clear, however, that such high death rates are due primarily to resistance being lessened by malnutrition. At least half the human race lives in want and cannot obtain enough food with the proper content of proteins, fats, minerals, and vitamins.

The British agricultural expert Robert Allaby has said that the human race already had their backs to the wall with regard to food supplies midway through the 'sixties. Since 1958 food production in the underdeveloped countries has no longer been able to keep pace with population growth, and food has been transported by the rich nations, especially the United States. Crop failures in the developed countries in 1965 and 1966 were the first major defeat in the fight against hunger. In 1972 and 1973 poor harvests caused by adverse weather throughout the world trebled world market food prices. Many developing countries were, of course, the victims. Even the U.N. food conference held in Rome in 1974 because of the emergency offered few prospects for the world's hungry.

The rich industrialised nations, which together house 30 percent of the world's population, not only produce over half the food, but consume it as well. This means that 70 percent have to make do with less than half the output. Of the few nations with food surpluses, the U.S., Canada, and Australia are by far the most important. But no speedy change seems likely to the present situation, in which surpluses are sold at normal market prices to countries that can pay for them. In order to keep pace with population growth on the one hand and at the same time to safeguard mankind in the near future against wholesale deaths from starvation, agricultural production will have to be stepped up, especially in developing territories. The possibilities of doing this will be gone into in the following sections.

3.2.2 Increase in arable land

The most obvious way of increasing food production appears to be to extend the existing area under cultivation. What is the position, and what possibilities are there?

Of the total surface of the earth – 50,800 million hectares – land accounts for 28.3 percent (14,500 million hectares). This land is subdivided as follows: 11 percent arable land, 19 percent grassland, 30 percent forest, and 40 percent with no vegetation (polar regions, deserts, mountains, and so on).

We therefore now have about 1,600 million hectares of arable land, and any new agricultural land will have to be taken from existing grassland and forests. Since natural grassland is not usually suitable for conversion into arable land, we are dependent mainly on the clearance of forests. But we obviously cannot simply go on felling trees. Forests are not only a major source of self-replenishing raw materials; they are also of vital ecological importance. They consist of highly complex, well-balanced, natural communities and are indispensable in maintaining the oxygen balance. The high productivity of tropical forests indicates the existence of a favourable climate and a rich soil structure. In the past, however, practically every attempt to turn such areas into arable land has failed, because when the growth was removed the soil could not stand the heavy rainfalls. The annual loss of topsoil through erosion may be as much as 600 cubic metres per hectare. This means that even the very best farming cannot keep the soil productive for more than 20 years, and in many regions for even less than five. Research by the U.N. Food and Agriculture Organisation (F.A.O. 1970) indicates that some newly obtained arable land would have to be turned into grazing land again to stop it deteriorating into desert.

Buringh, Van Heemst, and Staring (1975) estimate the maximum area theoretically suitable for agriculture at 3,387 million hectares, or 25 percent of the earth's land surface. More realistic estimates are a possible increase to 2,800-3,200 million hectares. But we must bear in mind that the most fertile land is already being used for farming and that these estimates include less suitable marginal land. According to the F.A.O. report mentioned above, it is already virtually impossible to extend the existing acreage on economic grounds.

3.2.3 The green revolution

A second possibility for fighting world hunger is to increase the yield from existing arable land. The developed countries have been doing this for a long time by means of very intensive farming. The highly industrialised methods involved, however, put it beyond the reach of developing countries; so this is not the answer.

Hence a solution has been sought by developing high-yielding varieties of grain and rice. Experiments have concentrated on cultivating quick-growing strains with large ears and short stems allowing several crops to be harvested each year. In 1970 Norman Borlaug was awarded the Nobel Peace prize for his work in this field. The Nobel Commitee described it as 'a breakthrough in grain production, which will make it possible to expel hunger from developing regions within a few years.' René Dubos and Barbara Ward, in their book *Only one earth*, strongly support this 'Green Revolution'. They recommend growing high-yielding grains to remedy the distress in the hungry regions of the world.

The results have indeed been striking. Grain varieties have been developed which can ripen in 120 days instead of 150 and which can tolerate fertilisation with over 130 kilograms of nitrogen per hectare. A new rice variety has given 10 times the yield in experimental paddy-fields; this was achieved by harvesting three times a year and using nearly 300 kilograms of fertiliser per hectare. But it has meanwhile become clear that the views of the Nobel Committee and the name 'Green Revolution' are both very optimistic indeed. The changes in the genetic characteristics of the varieties that were used have also produced a number of adverse properties. A major drawback of the new varieties is the heavy fertilisation their production involves. It is very doubtful whether the developing countries can provide this. Other drawbacks are lower resistance to disease and a deterioration in structure and protein content of the grain. Moreover, it mostly takes about 10 years for the favourable characteristics of a new variety to become stabilised and permanent. This seems a very long time against the background of the rapidly increasing world food shortage.

The conviction that the 'Green Revolution' will soon provide an answer has been overtaken by events. But let us hope that results so far will suffice to alleviate the most crying needs in the years ahead.

Conclusions and principles for a model

The food situation of the future depends on a great diversity of factors and is hardly predictable, if at all. Optimists believe we may be able to maintain the present situation for another 20 years or so at its existing (inadequate) level. Linneman (1976) considers it will be possible to increase food production by the years 2010 to two and a half times its present level. Pessimists, however, are convinced that a serious famine is just around the corner. Present trends unfortunately suggest that the pessimists will be right.

Diets also demand attention. People in the prosperous countries often eat and drink too much. Eating more meat than the normal protein requirement (50-100 grams a day) means that food is being consumed unnecessarily, since on average seven kilograms of grain are needed to produce one kilogram of meat. Then there are the vast amounts of meat devoured by cats and dogs. A proper diet can bring about big savings.

Having regard to the presumed success of birth control measures, it will be assumed in the model that food production will be able to keep up with the limited population growth. The doubts about the possibilities of the 'Green Revolution' necessitate a substantial increase in arable land.

3.3 Natural resources

The earth provides a wide range of natural resources. They can be subdivided into two categories (Table 3.1):
1. materials which, if at all, are produced by the earth exceedingly slowly;
2. materials produced by the earth from year to year, such as timber, flax, cotton, cane and rushes.

The former category can again be divided into two groups: resources in limited supply (energy sources, metals, and so on) and those in ample supply (stone, sand, lime, and so on).

In view of the objectives of the study, the choice and treatment of resources was based particularly on those of importance as building materials.

Table 3.1. Some important materials in the building industry

Non-renewable resources		Produced from year to year by the earth
Limited resources	Ample resources	
Steel	stone	timber
Aluminium	sand	flax
Copper	gravel, chippings	cotton
Lead	lime, gypsum	cane and rushes
Zinc	cement	cork
Fossil fuels:	bricks (clay)	rubber
coal	sandstone	
oil	concrete	
natural gas	glass	

Principles for a model

This study is based on present known world reserves. Future exploration will no doubt prove the reserves to be greater. New recovery methods are also likely to

increase exploitable quantities of materials. It is therefore possible to adopt higher norms for permissible consumption than would otherwise have been the case.

Before natural resources reach the point of consumption as materials, a whole sequence of operations is required: recovery, transport, conversion, and so on. Each stage uses up materials and energy. When materials are used in practice, therefore, many kinds of resources are drawn upon. The discussion of individual resources below gives a brief description in each case of the conversion process and the energy it consumes. The pollution caused by a number of processes is also indicated (see 3.5).

As regards the permissible consumption of natural resources, an arbitrary decision had to be taken. It was decided to take a permitted annual consumption of not more than 1 percent of the reserves available at the beginning of the year. If no new reserves become available, this means that less and less can be used from year to year. Hence, after twenty-five years 77.8 percent of the original reserves is left, after fifty years 60.5 percent, after seventy-five years 47.1 percent and after a hundred years 36.5 percent. As the permitted amount thus continues decreasing, the reserves are never completely exhausted. Nevertheless, it hardly seems justifiable to use up 63.5 percent of all the resources in limited supply in the next hundred years. It should be noted however:

1. that present known reserves are bound to be replenished owing to new or improved prospecting and recovery methods;
2. that the limitation relates only to *recovery* of the materials. Consumption can be cut down by greater recycling;
3. that in the course of time new substitutes may be developed as less of the originals becomes available.

To recapitulate: it was decided to take the permissible consumption of scarce resources as 1 percent of known reserves, combined with the present level of recycling and the present knowledge of possible alternatives. This norm is in keeping with the resolutions of the U.N. Conference in Stockholm referred to in Chapter 1.

As the materials most readily accessible will be recovered first, the cost of utilising new reserves will steadily increase.

3.3.1 Limited resources

Let us take in succession the various materials of importance in the building industry.

3.3.1.1 Steel

In housing, steel is the most widely used of all metals. It is used mainly for central heating installations, door and window frames, windows, and supporting structures.

If properly protected, a large proportion of the steel can be recycled. This is practically impossible for steel in reinforced concrete. With our present technology it is not yet an economic proposition to replace this iron on a large scale with other materials such as glass-fibre cables.

Steel is made by smelting iron ore to obtain pig iron. This process takes place in blast furnaces and uses large amounts of coke as fuel and reducing agent. The coke left in the form of slag after smelting is used by the cement industry as a material for blast-furnace cement. It is used in an expanded form as ground slag which forms insulating aggregate in concrete structures.

Besides the energy needed for the smelting process, considerable quantities are used for converting pig iron into steel and rolling it into commercial sections. Energy consumption is often expressed as kilograms coal equivalent (kg CE). One kg CE is the amount of energy released by burning one kg of coal (i.e. 7,000 kilogram-calories). The production of 1,000 kg of worked steel also requires 1,000 kg CE in energy.

Known reserves of iron ore in 1970 were equivalent to 100,000 million tonnes, while in the same year 420 million tonnes of iron were produced. If consumption remains unchanged, therefore, there will be sufficient ore for 240 years. But consumption is increasing exponentially with a growth rate of 1.8 percent per annum. At this rate, reserves will suffice for only another 93 years.

With a maximum consumption of 1 percent of available reserves, 1,000 million tonnes would be available in the first year, or much more than actual consumption in 1970. The model also indicates the future trend in permitted consumption.

3.3.1.2 Aluminium

After steel, aluminium is the metal most widely used in the building industry. It has several advantages over steel: its specific gravity is lower, it has greater corrosion resistance and is easy to make into sections. A drawback, however, is the much greater deformation by loads or major temperature fluctuations. In the building industry, the use of aluminium is increasing very rapidly (by an average of 10 percent a year).

The world has ample reserves of aluminium, and 8 percent of the earth's crust consists of it. But as a recoverable material only limited supplies are available. Known reserves in 1970 were about 1,170 million tonnes. World production that year was 11.7 million tonnes, and if consumption remains unchanged, there is sufficient for 100 years. With continued exponential growth, however, there will be enough for only 31 years.

Introduction of the norm of 1 percent of known reserves would allow 11.7 million tonnes for the first year. Consumption will therefore have to be gradually reduced. The principal aluminium ore (bauxite) deposits are in Jamaica, the Soviet Union, Surinam, France, and the U.S.

The first stage in the production of aluminium is a chemical process. With the aid of a caustic soda solution a pure aluminium hydroxide is obtained from the red, yellow, or grey bauxite. The second stage is to separate the metal from the hydroxide. This reducing process, which at present is carried out almost exclusively by electrolysis, uses very much energy. The aluminium production process, together with the energy consumption, is shown in Figure 3.1.

This process devours 4,200 kg CE per tonne. Recycling, however, requires much less. At present about 40 percent of the aluminium is recycled. As the technology of generating large amounts of energy is comparatively new, aluminium production has only a short history. Production only really got under way after the invention of the electric furnace in 1886.

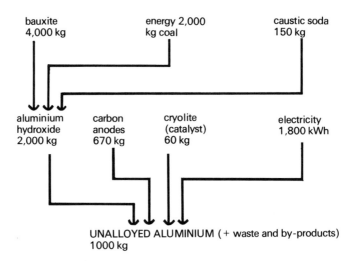

Figure 3.1. The aluminium production process

Only countries with large amounts of energy at their disposal are major aluminium producers. The Netherlands has produced aluminium since the great natural gas discoveries. But natural energy sources are regarded as unable to meet all the steadily growing demand for electric power. A solution is now being sought primarily in the use of nuclear energy. A striking example of these developments is the aluminium project in Zeeuws-Vlaanderen and the nuclear power plant at Borssele, Holland.

3.3.1.3 Copper

The high price of copper has greatly reduced its use as a building material, except in electrical installations. To replace copper as a conductor, small-scale experiments are being made with water-filled plastic tubing.

Although copper occurs naturally in a pure form, it is mainly recovered from ore. Copper ore is mined mainly in the U.S. and Chile, which together possess 40 percent of world reserves. There are also large reserves in Zambia. Like steel and aluminium, copper is very suitable for recycling: about 21 percent is at present re-used.

Known world reserves in 1970 were equivalent to 308 million tonnes, and will be exhausted in 36 years at the present rate of consumption. With an exponential growth rate, they will last only 21 years.

The norm of using 1 percent of known reserves would provide only 3 million tonnes in the first year. The 1970 consumption of 8.5 million tonnes shows how precarious the situation was even then. The international tension to which such situations can give rise was reflected in the intervention by the U.S. in Chile and by France in Zaire. Proper husbanding of resources can ensure that the use of copper is avoided wherever possible.

Copper is extracted by grinding and then roasting rich ores. The resulting impure copper is reduced with charcoal and then refined to a high degree of purity (98-99 percent). The slag, the residue from the roasting process, is converted, for instance, into copper stone-slag and is widely used in road construction and for decorative paving. Copper production is a high-energy process: 2,450 kg CE is needed per 1,000 kg.

3.3.1.4 Lead

Lead plays a modest part in the building process. It is used for sealing, for watertight flashings, for wastepipes, and so on. It is also the basic material for red lead production. In recent years lead has been increasingly replaced by petroleum products such as bitumen felt and plastics. Lead is very toxic: in drinking water as little as 0.1 ppm is harmful.

In 1970 known world reserves were 91 million tonnes, while world production was 3.5 million. If consumption continues at this rate, therefore, there is sufficient for another 26 years. But the increase in lead consumption is also exponential, and known reserves will thus be exhausted in 21 years. The 1 percent norm would provide only 900,000 tonnes in the first year. The 1970 figures therefore show that consumption will have to be slashed. In view of the harmful side-effects lead has on human beings and the environment this can only be an improvement.

Lead is obtained by smelting galena; the reaction is:

$$2PbS + SO_2 \rightarrow 2PbO + 2SO_2 \uparrow$$

The production of 1,000 kg lead requires about 1,850 kg CE.

3.3.1.5 Zinc

Zinc is no longer a widely used building material: it is used mainly for gutters, roofing dormer windows, and so on. The decline is due mainly to the effects of air pollution. Especially in industrial areas, the high sulphur content of the atmosphere corrodes zinc quickly. In the past 50 years the useful life of zinc has been more than halved (to 10 or 15 years). By contrast, its use as a protective plating for steel has greatly increased and takes as much as 30 to 40 percent of the total world production. In this galvanising process, a thin coating of zinc is applied to steel by dipping or spraying, to provide a corrosion-resistant surface. If this zinc coating is then protected with paint as well, a life of 25 to 30 years is quite possible. Like lead, zinc uses about 1,850 kg CE per tonne.

The consumption of zinc in 1970 was about 5.4 million tonnes. Known reserves are 123 million tonnes, or sufficient for 23 years if consumption remains unchanged. The estimated growth in consumption is 2.9 percent per annum, and this makes the reserves sufficient for 18 years. With the 1 percent norm, 1.2 million tonnes would be available in the first year, or only a proportion of actual consumption in 1970. We shall therefore have to seek other means of protection and also reduce consumption.

3.3.1.6 *Plastics*

The principal primary materials for plastics are petroleum and coal; a small proportion of cellulose is also used. Their conversion into plastics involves highly complex chemical processes. World plastics production in 1972 was estimated at 30 million tonnes with a total petroleum production of 2,500 million tonnes. Of all fossil fuels recovered (oil, coal, and natural gas), only 1 percent is used for plastics production.

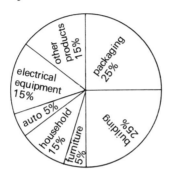

Figure 3.2. Plastics' consumption, sector-wise.

Figure 3.2 shows the importance of plastics in the building industry. The Netherlands uses more plastics for housing than any other European country (average 36 kg per housing unit in 1972). Approximately 65 percent of the total is accounted for by wastepipes and 20 percent for electrical circuits and insulation. The use of plastics is expected to increase further in the next few years. An attractive aspect is their use as insulating materials to reduce energy losses. Another important aspect is that they make it possible to save other scarce materials. Table 3.2 shows the potential saving in the Soviet Union (I.V. Rakhlin and L. I. Koshkin, 1972).

Table 3.2. Potential saving of traditional materials by using plastics (U.S.S.R., 1975)

Material	Saving in tonnes
Cast iron	153×10^3
Steel	252×10^3
Aluminium	186×10^3
Copper ⎫ Lead ⎬ Zinc ⎭	$1,536 \times 10^3$
Timber	$7,273 \times 10^3$

Table 3.3. Basic material consumption, water pollution, and energy consumption per tonne of low-density polyethylene granules

Process	Consumption of petroleum as basic material (tonnes)	Water pollution (population equivalents)	Consumption of petroleum as energy (tonnes)
Distillation of naphtha from petroleum	1.41	0.0011	0.03
Ethylene production from naphta	1.38	0.0043	0.36
Polymerisation of ethylene to LDPE	1.05	hardly any	0.29
Total	3.84	0.0054	0.70

Thus, although there are advantages in using plastics, they also cause pollution. Water pollution is expressed in population equivalents (PE), the biological oxygen demand (BOD) caused by domestic waste-water per inhabitant in 24 hours, with a break-down period of five days and at a water temperature of 20°C; one PE is assumed to correspond to 54 grams BOD.

Table 3.3 gives the basic material consumption, water pollution, and energy per tonne of low density polyethylene granules (Schuur, 1973). The figures for PVC, the plastic most widely used in houses, are: petroleum as basic material 0.7 tonnes, water pollution 0.105 PE, and energy 1.2 tonnes of petroleum.

The Netherlands' aggregate plastics' production in 1971 was some 400,000 tonnes, resulting in a BOD of surface water of about 1,000 tonnes. This seems fairly low, considering that the country's aggregate BOD from industrial processes was 2.6 million tonnes (in 1971). Plastics' production thus causes only 0.04 percent of the total BOD. Criticism of plastics from this angle is therefore not always justified. A more important problem is their very poor biodegradability. Products do now exist which degrade fairly quickly in the open air, but they are not, of course, suitable for use as durable materials.

3.3.2 Ample resources

Ample resources obviously cause fewer problems than limited resources; there is no need to ascertain the reserves or restrict their use.

But it is still relevant to ask what their recovery and production involves and how this affects the environment. If limited resources (including energy) are used to obtain them, this will draw on the quantities allowed by the 1 percent norm. Pollution will also have to be kept within the specified limits. The principle resources are discussed below.

3.3.2.1 Stone, sand, gravel, and chippings

In building houses, sand and gravel are used mainly as aggregates in mortars (cement mortar, bricklaying mortar, plaster, and so on). Although there is practically no scarcity, if any at all, of these materials worldwide, regional shortages may occur. In Western Europe, for instance, fresh-water sand is being used up, but saline sand can be desalinated fairly easily, and this is already a common practice. In the case of these materials, therefore, the emphasis is on the energy consumed in their recovery and transport, and on the consequent pollution of soil, air, and water. Energy consumption is low: about 1 kg CE per 1,000 kg product.

3.3.2.2 Lime, gypsum, and cement

Lime is obtained mainly by burning limestone, as a result of which the carbonic acid is driven off and unslaked lime is formed. After soaking in water, a binder is obtained suitable for incorporating in mortar and plaster.

Burning, slaking, and setting involve the following reactions:

burning: $CaCO_3 \rightarrow CaO + CO_2 - 42.5$ cal.

slaking: $CaO + H_2O \rightarrow Ca(OH)_2 + 15.5$ cal.

setting: $Ca(OH)_2 + CO_2 \rightarrow CaCO_3 + H_2O$

Comparatively large amounts of carbon dioxide (CO_2) are released and are largely discharged into the atmosphere (about 500 kg CO_2 per 1,000 kg product). Energy consumption is 215 kg CE per 1,000 kg product.

Gypsum is used in the building industry mainly as a binder in plasters and also for making light-weight partitions. It is a water-soluble, corrosive material which attacks iron. It is manufactured by heating anhydrous calcium sulphate, $CaSO_4 \cdot 2H_2O$, occurring as a mineral, to drive off water of crystallisation. It sets by absorbing water from the mixture, so that the original calcium sulphate reappears.

Cement is the most important hydraulic binder of all. It is used in large quantities in cement mortar, bricklaying mortar, and so on.

Cement was known to the Romans. A mixture of calcined lime and hydraulic pozzuolana, the *Roman cement*, was no longer used after the end of the Roman Empire. It was not until 1846 that it was again possible to produce a strong hydraulic binder: Portland cement.

The principal material in cement manufacture is clay containing silica (SiO_2) and aluminium oxide (Al_2O_3). To improve quality, pyrite ash containing about 85 percent F_2O_3 is added. The cement is obtained by calcinating, sintering, and grinding.

Production of 1,000 kg of cement takes 170 kg CE. It affects the environment; about 500 kg CO/CO_2 is produced per 1,000 kg cement. On top of this, the quarrying away of hills like the St. Pietersberg in Limburg, Holland, often spoils the countryside.

3.3.2.3 Burnt brick and sand-lime brick

In regions where there are plenty of natural clay deposits, burnt bricks have been one of the most widely used building materials since ancient times. In the Netherlands, for instance, they are used for practically all the outside walls of terraced houses. In times of scarcity, for instance shortly after the Second World War, bricks increasingly replaced timber. Wooden beams and floors have been superseded by reinforced hollow-brick floors. Other burnt-clay products, such as wall and flooring tiles and washbasins, are used in practically all homes.

A comparatively new product is the sand-lime brick. This is not burnt but is made by compressing a mixture of damp sand with slaked lime, forming a chemical compound with a uniform consistency. The manufacture of burnt bricks uses considerably more energy than sand-lime bricks: 1,000 kg brick or tiles takes an average of 150 kg CE.

Bricklaying is a very labour-intensive building method. Consequently, there is a movement from traditional types of brick to materials requiring less labour.

3.3.2.4 Concrete

Concrete is a very widely used building material for blocks of flats. It is a mixture of cement, sand, and gravel (or other aggregate) which hardens, after the addition of water, to a stone-like mass. But after hardening, it can hardly absorb any tensile forces, and where such forces are liable to occur it is reinforced with steel in order to offset this structural drawback. The scarcity of steel therefore implies that the use of reinforced concrete should also be limited (see 3.3.1.1).

Concrete manufacture causes comparatively little pollution, and the energy consumption is low: 25 CE per 1,000 kg.

3.3.2.5 Glass

Its many valuable properties make glass virtually indispensable for modern housing. It was known in ancient Egypt: there is a 4,500 year-old drawing of glassblowers in a rock-cut tomb at Beni Hassan.

Glass is made by fusing quartz sand. Small amounts of other substances are added to the molten glass to improve its quality. Calcium, magnesium, and aluminium make the glass weatherproof and water-insoluble. Arsenic and manganese dioxide remove discoloration and make the glass bright and clear.

Although there is no shortage of the basic material, sand, glass is largely recycled because the manufacturing process requires a proportion of broken waste glass (cullet) to ensure good quality.

Glass manufacture, formerly craftwork, is now a fully industrial process. The production of huge sheets is no longer a technical problem, and large windows are widely used in modern architecture with, of course, a major effect on domestic energy consumption. Glass has very poor insulating properties, with big energy losses. Double glazing is a means of limiting these (see Appendix D).

Glass production takes about 700 kg CE per 1,000 kg. Atmospheric pollution is caused mainly by carbon dioxide and sulphur dioxide.

3.3.3 Resources produced by the earth from year to year

A plant's viability is governed by two principal factors:
1. the total amount of solar energy with which it is irradiated for photosynthesis;
2. the local conditions where the solar energy is received. These can be im-

proved, for instance by irrigation and crop rotation. Deforestation causing soil erosion and overcropping have a contrary effect.

Food production was discussed extensively in 3.2; let us now take timber, as a
major material for building living accommodation.

3.3.3.1 Timber

Wood has been a major material for building houses since ancient times,
mainly because of its versatility; it is suitable not only for constructional
functions – supporting walls, floors, and roofs – but also for nearly all the
accessories – door and window frames, doors, inside and outside wall covering, and even as a roofing material. Its durability can be greatly improved by a
number of preserving methods; if properly used and maintained, it will retain
its properties for a very long time. The many different kinds of wood all have
specific properties regarding composition, structure, hardness, strength,
durability, and their relevant uses.

The natural structure and grain of the worked surface and the infinite range
of colours make wood of great esthetic value.

In contrast to most other materials for building houses, timber has the
advantage of needing comparatively little energy for recovery and conversion. Pollution is also negligible. Forests, in fact, make a very substantial
contribution to maintenance of the ecosystem, since they discharge vast
amounts of oxygen into the atmosphere. They also have many other functions, such as providing food for man and animals. They prevent soil erosion
and have a favourable effect on climate and soil conditions. Lastly, they have
a social function as recreational areas.

Pollution may be caused when wood is used in practice, especially through
the use of preservatives.

3.3.3.2 World reserves and annual consumption

Wood differs from other major building materials in that the reserves are self-
replenishing. A higher yield can be obtained by increasing production per
square kilometre, and/or by extending the existing area of forest.

As regards the potential extension of forests, this is obviously related directly to the problem of food supplies. We have seen in Chapter 3 that the
present tragic position of world food supplies demands not only agricultural
improvements where possible but also the extension of existing arable land.

This will be all the more necessary if cutting down on fertilisers and pesticides reduces the yield per hectare. Space will also have to be kept for non-food products such as cotton, flax, cane, and rushes. Hence, there is limited scope for timber production.

Of the 43.4 million sq.km of woodland and forests we now have 13.2 million are used for timber production. Per sq.km there is approximately 9,000 cu.m of usable timber, bringing effective world reserves to 120 billion cu.m: 64 billion softwood and 56 billion hardwood. Annual timber consumption in 1969 was 2.1 billion cu.m. The ways in which it was used are given in Table 3.4.

Table 3.4. World timber consumption (1969)

Use	World 10^6 m^3	%	U.S. 10^6 m^3	%	Africa 10^6 m^3	%
Structural timber	774	36.1	205	61.2	14	6.1
Paper, pulp	277	12.9	96	28.4	1	0.4
Others	161	7.5	15	4.3	10	4.1
Fuel	933	43.5	20	6.1	212	89.4
Total fellings	2,145	100	336	100	237	100

To illustrate the contrasting patterns of consumption, the U.S. and Africa are shown separately. It is striking how much wood is still used for fuel, especially in the developing countries. Nevertheless, its proportion in world energy supplies has decreased greatly. From 57 percent in 1860 and 13 percent in 1913 it had fallen to 3.5 percent by 1953. We can therefore assume that in the future the developing countries will also use less wood as fuel.

The average output per sq.km is now 180 cu.m per annum. Van der Meiden (1971) says that on most soils in temperate regions an output of 1,000 cu.m per sq.km is possible, and in tropical regions even more. Taking an average annual output of 1,000 cu.m/sq.km, therefore, an annual production of 13 billion cu.m could be attained by retaining the present acreage and intensifying afforestation. Browning (1963) says that 30 million sq.km of the existing forest can be exploited economically. This means that with an annual yield of 1,000 cu.m per sq.km it would even be possible to produce 30 billion cu.m a year.

Despite these theoretical possibilities we must not be over-optimistic about future timber production. On the one hand, the big demand for timber as an industrial material has led to overcropping in many places, so that the average

age at which trees are felled is falling steadily. On the other hand, extensive areas are still being deforested throughout the world to provide space for arable land. According to the F.A.O., 600 sq.km of forest is disappearing in this way every day. It has been found in the past that this has frequently led to soil impoverishment and erosion. Arable land obtained in this way is often productive for only 20 years, and in moist, temperate zones it takes about 200 years before abandoned farmland turns into forest again.

A final point: spraying with chemical defoliants during the Vietnam War turned over 400,000 hectares of forest into barren land. The long-term effects of such action are incalculable.

Conclusions and principles for a model

Notwithstanding the wide scope that exists in theory for stepping up timber production without adversely affecting food production, energy consumption, and the environment, consumption will still have to be controlled.

The model assumes that a production of 700 cu.m per sq.km forest can be obtained by improved forestry methods. Against this, the economically exploitable area will be reduced in favour of housing and food supplies. The permissible limit for timber consumption is taken as equal to the annual growth of timber, and there are thus no additional withdrawals from reserves.

3.4 Energy

For many centuries the only alternatives to manpower were wood-fires, waterwheels, and windmills. The industrial revolution changed all that. The arrival of the steam engine saw the use of huge amounts of coal. This era also came to an end. The steam engine was superseded by the internal combustion engine, bringing a demand for a different fuel: motor spirit. One oilfield after another was exploited. But events have moved so fast that now petroleum is no longer an adequate energy source.

Table 3.5 gives the distribution of gross energy consumption by various sectors in the E.E.C. Intensive efforts are being made to develop alternative energy sources: nuclear energy, solar energy, wind and water power, tidal power, energy from melting ice, temperature gradients, geothermal energy, and energy from organic waste. The extent to which it has been possible to make these alternative sources operational will be discussed in 3.4.5. First, a brief description of the three most important fossil fuels: coal, petroleum (including tar sands and shale), and natural gas.

Table 3.5. Gross energy consumption per sector (E.E.C.)

Sector	1955 %	1969 %	1980 %
Steel industry	13.4	10.4	7.1
Other manufacturing industries	28.5	25.9	25.7
Transport	12.6	12.1	14.1
Households	26.1	29.2	30.4
Energy	10.6	3.9	2.7
Shipping	2.7	4.6	4.9
Energy as material	0.1	6.2	8.5
Losses in transport	2.3	1.5	1.5
Losses in transformation	3.7	6.2	5.1

3.4.1 Coal

For a long time coal was the most important fossil fuel. Its consumption reached a peak in the days of the steam engine, the steam train, and the steamboat.

Although the use of coal has steadily declined, a turning point may now have been reached. In opencast-mining countries (U.S., U.S.S.R., China, South Africa, and Australia) there is now a big increase in production, unlike Western Europe with its very high-cost deep mining.

World coal reserves were estimated in 1970 at 5×10^{12} tonnes. But large quantities of these are in not easily accessible places. In the same year, world production was 2.2×10^9 tonnes. If consumption remains unchanged, therefore, supplies are sufficient for over 2,300 years.

Energy can be obtained from coal in various ways: by burning, conversion into gas or petrol. So far burning is the most extensive method. Conversion into gas (in coke ovens) is also widely applied. This method practically disappeared in the Netherlands since the discovery of natural gas, but has recently come into the picture again. Conversion of coal into oil and petrol dates from the 'twenties (in Germany). The coal was hydrated, i.e. hydrogen was added to the carbon atoms in the form of the deuterium isotope.

Recent research has produced more effective and ecologically harmless methods. Experiments are being made, for instance, with direct gasification of coal in the mine. The advantages are obvious. The gas is easier to transport, and very deep and inaccessible coal seams can be "worked". Coal is therefore likely to take a bigger place in energy consumption than it has done in the last few decades.

3.4.2 Petroleum

Besides coal, petroleum is the most widely used fossil fuel. Partly because of its relatively simple and cheap recovery and easy transport, the use of petroleum and petroleum products has grown tremendously.

World petroleum reserves (including tar sands and shale) were estimated in 1970 at 58 billion tonnes, while consumption was 1.9 billion. As consumption is increasing exponentially, known reserves will probably be exhausted in twenty years' time. In view of the many possible superior uses, it is wasteful to burn oil and it will have to be avoided wherever possible.

In the highly industrialised E.E.C., the proportion of petroleum in overall energy consumption increased from 24 percent in 1955 to 62 percent in 1969, while 65 percent is expected in 1980. It need hardly be explained, therefore, why regions with petroleum reserves are at the focal point of political attention.

The oil producing and exporting countries joined together in O.P.E.C. in 1960. Their objectives are to obtain higher prices and a bigger share in oil production. The Tripoli and Teheran agreements (1971) are well known in this connection. After the oil crisis of 1973/74 it became clear that, besides oil, natural gas was also going to become a major factor in energy supplies.

3.4.3 Natural gas

Streets were lit for the first time with coal gas about 1800. This was a mixture of hydrogen, methane, and carbon monoxide. It was in full use until 1950, after which it was gradually superseded by natural gas.

Natural gas (methane, CH_4) supplies nearly twice as many calories as coal gas. It is easy to recover, needs no refining, and is easy to transport. Pipelines are used for short distances. Liquefied, it can be carried in tankers over long distances and in huge quantities. Each cubic metre is then equal to 600 cu.m of gas. A 50,000-tonne tanker can carry as much as 30 million cubic metres of gas, sufficient for a year's consumption by a city with 100,000 inhabitants.

In 1970 estimated world reserves of natural gas were 3×10^{13} cu.m, and the annual consumption was 8×10^{11} cu.m; these quantities have meanwhile almost doubled. In 1955 the proportion of natural gas in overall energy supplies was only 1 percent and in 1969 7 percent; it is expected to reach 13 percent by 1980.

3.4.4 Alternative energy sources

Nuclear energy

When it became possible to control the flow of energy released by splitting the atom, many people were imbued with fantastic ideas. They envisaged ships capable of sailing for over a year with fuel supplies of only some tens of kilograms. They imagined power stations well able to meet the increasing demand for energy. And they thought of weapons with inconceivable destructive power due to the vast amount of energy. Everything has proved true. Ships are sailing with nuclear propulsion, there are nuclear power stations, and there are terrifying nuclear weapons.

In nuclear fission the nuclei of uranium (a heavy, silvery metal) are split with the aid of neutrons in a controlled chain reaction. This fission produces energy in the form of heat, which is mostly used to raise steam. Even though nuclear energy has been used for some decades, it is in fact still in the experimental stage. There are countless unsolved problems. For instance, it is still practically impossible to dismantle a nuclear power station out of operation. What are we going to do with all those hundreds of power stations the world already has? Another problem is that of radioactive waste. So far, it has mainly been dumped at sea, but this is obviously not an ideal solution at all. There are already alarming reports of increased radioactivity in the seawater near the dumping sites. There is, moreover, a risk of sabotage at the power stations, theft, and misuse of the fissile materials. And then there is practically no solution to the problem of thermal pollution by discharged cooling water.

Solar energy

An important alternative energy source already employed on a modest scale is that of solar energy. Solar radiation can be used in various ways. For instance: conversion into heat with collectors or concave mirrors, direct conversion into electricity with solar cells, and the use of photosynthesis to grow trees for fuel. A problem with solar energy is that it is not always obtained and used in one and the same place, and it thus has to be transported. A good method is dialysis of water. This process releases gaseous hydrogen which can be burnt again elsewhere after transportation. Dialysis is a clean process.

Research is at present being carried out into the possibility of collecting solar radiation in space and sending the energy to the earth via a laser beam. This is still in its initial stages.

Windpower

A traditional alternative energy source is windpower. It has been used through the ages. Sails carried ships across the seas; windmills ground the grain, sawed the wood, and drained the polders. The use of windpower fell into disuse when machines that did not have to rely on the wind became available.

It is now drawing attention again. Studies have been made which show that in temperate zones large windpower stations can be built out at sea. The size of the mills, however, would make them of incidental importance only.

Waterpower

Power generation by means of falling or fast-running water is already fairly widely employed. Possibilities differ from country to country. They are made greater by damming rivers. The unwelcome side-effects this may have were referred to in the introduction.

Another form of waterpower is the ever-changing level between high and low tides. For effective utilisation, the difference has to be at least four to five metres. In Brittany in France a 340-megawatt station is at present operating on this principle. The investment per watt is high.

Theoretically, the currents of melting ice water in the polar regions can be used to generate electricity. In these regions the change of seasons is accompanied by enormous transformations of water into ice and vice versa. This ensures an absolutely clean, very even, and most reliable energy source. Another advantage is that no cultivable land need be sacrified.

An experimental form of energy generation is the exploitation of the difference in temperature between the warm upper stratum of the sea and the deeper cold water. But this requires an expensive installation, while its efficiency is low on the basis of present methods. But the potential capacity of this source is considerable. The warm Gulf Stream off the coast of Florida could alone supply enough energy each year to cover four times America's 1970 energy requirements.

Geothermal energy

This alternative energy source is used occasionally. In 1970, the installed capacity was about 10^9 watts.

The temperature of the earth's crust rises steadily towards the core (by about 1°C per 31 metres). The heat existing at great depths is usable. In Iceland this is a natural process. Many homes in Reykjavik are centrally heated with hot water rising out of the ground.

Though the potential reserves are large, complications may occur in their utilisation. The output, and not the potential reserve, is the ultimate criterion. Thermal studies by Carnot and others show that an energy source can supply only part of its energy in the form of work. The ratio between energy (E) and work (A) is:

$$A = E\,(1 - \frac{T_2}{T_1}),$$

in which T_1 is the absolute temperature of the energy source and T_2 the ambient temperature (the temperature at which work is used). This ratio indicates the maximum work available from an unloaded energy source. It can then be calculated that for each process in which energy is irreversibly converted into work the efficiency will be a maximum of 50 percent.

Because of the importance of factor A, the name 'exergy' was proposed for it in 1953 but did not become widely used. If we apply this notion to geothermal energy we find it to be very poor in exergy. Only 20 percent of the energy supplied to the earth's surface can be usefully employed; the other 80 percent is lost in the form of heat. And this means that the largescale use of geothermal energy would greatly increase thermal pollution, with all its consequences. Its use will therefore have to remain limited. But it is suitable for heating purposes.

Organic waste

Lastly, an alternative energy form widely used in countries such as India and Iran: the recovery of energy from organic waste. Oil or methane gas can be obtained from waste by chemical or bacteriological means. The method is particularly suitable for supplying the energy requirements of small users.

Conclusions and principles for the model

There are vast fossil fuel reserves, especially in the form of coal. But many of these can hardly be utilised, if at all, at the present time. It has also been found that there are large potential reserves of several alternative energy sources but that their exploitation is still at an experimental stage. There is unlikely to be any change in this in the near future.

For this reason it was decided to keep the proportion of energy obtained from alternative sources constant at the 1970 level. This implies that their use will grow at the same rate as energy consumption as a whole. Owing to the substitutability of the various energy sources, there is no point in introducing a limit to consumption for each individual category. Hence only the overall annual consumption was limited to 1% of present reserves. But it may nevertheless be wise to allow for the most efficient use of these energy sources; thermal pollution will then have to be kept to a minimum.

3.5 Pollution of the environment

Man as a biological being is totally dependent on living nature. It is the source of all his food: he is part of the natural (eco)system. Under the pressure of nature's threats he has used his intelligence to cultivate nature in order to survive.

But not only this. Modern Western man, in order to meet his seemingly unlimited needs (especially material ones), has developed a technology and built up an industrial society, characterised by exponential growth, which is laying more and more claim to natural resources. It is becoming clearer and clearer that this is happening largely at the expense of the natural environment.

It is interesting to see that the Hopi Indian tradition already reflects a profound appreciation of the distressing situation (cf. Clear Creek, number 13, 1972). In their vision, the animals and plants, the eagles and people are all kept alive through the power of the flow of Nation. The interaction between all living things – the relation of rocks to land, the flow of water, the dance of yellow butterflies in the cornfields – all this marks the balance of Nature. It goes on:

> It seems that many of our people are falling for the new plans that come to us from Washington, plans which say that we should take our mineral resources out of Mother Earth and thereby accumulate money with which to buy more land. This to me is a very foolish thing to do because this is already our land. We cannot buy it again with the very thing that comes out of it. To buy and sell land is not right in the sight of our Great Spirit (From Andrew Hermequaftewa, a traditional Hopi).

3.5.1 Causes, effects, extent, and increase

In recent years pollution of the environment as a world-embracing problem has emerged harshly and clearly. Not only symptoms universally perceived, such as the over-familiar fogs and smogs and extensive fields of poison sea-weed along the Californian coast, but also many cases of mass destruction of certain species of animals and symptoms of poisoning among large groups of people demand our attention. The recent events in Seveso, Italy, are fresh in our minds.

It is also being realised that the consequences are not only of local but also of world significance. The world's climate is in danger of being changed by the higher concentrations of carbon dioxide and particulate matter in the atmosphere. The oceans are being polluted with organic matter, metal compounds, and other persistent waste such as pesticides that accumulate in the food chain.

It has become clear that pollution is threatening the entire system of life on earth. There is no need to give a detailed analysis of the many kinds of pollution, their sources, concentrations, and potential effects. It should suffice for present purposes to mention a few things which will once again emphasise the seriousness of the problem. In 1969 30,000 to 100,000 auks and guillemots died in the Irish Sea within a matter of weeks for no apparent reason. Detailed investigations showed the cause of death to be a combination of factors. The birds' tissues were found to contain high concentrations of many persistent toxic substances such as lead, mercury, selenium, arsenic, cadmium, chlorinated hydrocarbons, and polychlorinated biphenyls. After losing strength through moulting and a brief period of storms in August, lack of food caused the toxic matter accumulated in the fatty tissues to be released. The birds died in September, when the weather was calm and there was plenty to eat.

The use of highly fungicidal organic mercury compounds, for instance in agriculture and the paper industry, has caused many disasters. It is now clear that they are much more harmful than the former inorganic mercury of mainly natural origin. For example, in 1971 it was discovered that methyl mercury in concentrations as low as 1 to 10 billion reduces the growth rate of plankton and could thus affect under-water life as a whole.

Mercury poisoning in human beings is often caused by inadvertently eating seed treated with mercury, which affects the central nervous system and causes paralysis, physical deformity, mental aberration, and abnormalities at birth. The principal victims among animals are seed-eating birds, birds of prey, livestock, and marine vertebrates. In Iraq in 1972 there was severe poisoning affecting human beings, livestock, and fish. The situation was so serious that the government ordered that any person dumping grain treated with mercury in the river would be shot dead on the spot.

The sensational poisoning in Minamata, Japan, killed 67 people and permanently disabled 330. In all, 10,000 Japanese were affected by what came to be known as the 'Minamata disease'. It was caused by the industrial discharge of large quantities of inorganic mercury, which is microbiologically converted in the seawater system into dimethyl mercury and then accumulates in the food chain. Some claimed that over half the fishing community in the vicinity were affected. The true course of events was only discovered some years after the first symptoms appeared. The incident was followed by others elsewhere in Japan.

Research into air-polluting substances in the Rijnmond region in Holland was carried out by Muller (1978). The escalation of the environment problem is also apparent from Table 3.6 (Commoner, 1971), which gives for a number of pollutants the percentage increase in the amounts discharged over a given period. It also states the increase in population in the same period. The increase in pollution is only attributable to population growth to a slight extent and is caused far more by advancing technology.

Table 3.6. Causes of pollution

Cause of pollution	Period	Percentage increase:	
		of population	of pollution
Nitrogenous, non-organic fertiliser	1949-69	34	648
Synthetic organic pesticides	1950-67	30	267
Detergent phosphates	1946-68	42	1,845
Lead compounds (automobiles)	1946-67	41	415
Nitrogen oxides (automobiles)	1946-67	41	630
Plastic beer bottles	1950-67	30	595

3.5.2 The significance of ecological equilibrium

If certain species vanish from a coherent biological system, its diversity is reduced. Natural systems behave more stably as diversity increases. Conversely, the disappearance of a link in the system reduces its stability. As the system's resistance to threats (diseases and pests) decreases, this weakens the position of the remaining species.

The large-scale introduction of monocultures and the production of large amounts of waste no longer degradable by natural means seriously disturb the natural equilibrium both locally and worldwide. This greatly impedes nature in its evolution, its creative capacity of providing greater and greater variety.

In the Netherlands, for instance, out of the original 1,400 species of higher plants, 50 have disappeared altogether and 120 have been reduced to fewer than five localities (Van der Maarel, 1971). Besides this, 250 species have become rare to very rare; over 50 percent of the domestic species are in danger of deterioriation or extinction. In the Rijnmond region half the orginal species are no longer to be found. Table 3.7 shows the changes from common to rare. Table 3.8 shows a similar impoverishment in Dutch fauna.

Table 3.7. Higher plants in the Netherlands

Degree of rarity	Number of species	
	1900	1970
Extremely rare	88	136
Very rare	134	216
Rare	176	205
Fairly rare	215	206
Fairly common	226	181
Common	347	260
Very common	207	145
Total existing	1393	1349
Total potential	1399	1399
Extinct	6	50

Table 3.8. Vertebrates in the Netherlands

	Period	Total number of species	Decline	Stable	Increase
Fishes	1950-70	43	31	9	3
Amphibians	1940-70	14	13	1	–
Reptiles	1940-70	8	8	–	–
Nesting birds	1960-70	162	59	60	43
Mammals	1950-70	56	33	20	3

3.5.3 Norms for permissibility of pollution

It is very difficult indeed to approach pollution numerically as an overall effect and to establish and assess its consequences worldwide. A solution is made more difficult by a complex of factors, the main ones being the following:

1. The many kinds of pollutants, each with its own characteristic, direct or indirect, spontaneous or gradual effects on the environment and health, make the investigation most complex. Besides this, the degree of pollution and its effects have been established for only a small number of substances. Combinations of substances, formed by chemical interactions after discharge into the atmosphere, are sometimes more harmful than the individual substances themselves.
2. Dispersion in the environment often means that the effects become evident far away from the sources of pollution, and the cause is then often difficult to trace. By contrast, concentrations of industry and traffic may cause serious hazards in the immediate vicinity but be of little significance worldwide.
3. Because of natural delays in ecological processes, the harmful effects on the environment only become evident after some time has elapsed. Consequently, the seriousness of the true situation at a given moment is often underestimated and the necessary countermeasures are taken too late.

As long as there is no clear knowledge of the consequences, the permissibility and establishment of a danger limit depend very much on subjective judgement. Should we go to the uttermost limit (if there be one) at which human life is still possible? If not, to what level should pollution be reduced, and what does this imply? In the past it was often assumed that pollution was harmless provided it was adequately dispersed. But it is now realised that complete dispersion is rarely possible. Apart from which, the process may sometimes take a very long time. After all, there is no dispersion at all in biological systems. On the contrary, there is a possibility of pollutants being reconcentrated in some organisms. Perhaps the earth's industrial production could still be stepped up considerably without having any really fatal effects on man's existence. But it is doubtful, to put it mildly, whether such a situation is one we could appreciate. For some time to come economic considerations will obviously play a major part in political decision-making.

In view of these problems, international norms for the permissibility of pollutants for the earth and its inhabitants are practically non-existent. The U.N. Conference on the Environment and Man in Stockholm in 1972 merely made a declaration of objectives and principles in a general sense; no definite agreements were made.

But we can choose between earning more at the expense of the environment or making do with less in exchange for a rich, balanced world in which to live. Let us seek an equilibrium based on the desirable environment, which takes other values into account.

3.5.4 Pollution caused by building

Like any other industrial process, the recovery and production of building materials also causes pollution by discharging pollutants and heating surface waters. Table 3.10 states the pollution caused by the production of a number of materials, especially discharges of dust and smoke, carbon monoxide and dioxide, fluorides, sulphur dioxide, nitrogen oxides, and hydrocarbons. Appendix A lists some air pollutants and their effects on health and the environment.

If enough information were available, it ought to be possible to make a quantitative approximation of overall pollution resulting from certain building operations, as can be done in the case of energy. But there are many factors that make such an analysis impracticable, as already shown in 3.5.3.

As housing uses mainly natural materials whose recovery and conversions use up little energy (such as brick, sand, gravel, concrete, and timber), it causes little pollution compared with more sophisticated industrial processes.

3.5.5 The cost of control

There will be no avoiding a catastrophe due to the increasing burden put on the environment if population and industrial production go on growing, because in many cases the cost of pollution control for a given industrial process increases greatly with the percentage of waste treated per unit of product. Meadows (1972) gives two examples which clearly show how the degree of pollution control and the consequent rise in costs are related.

1. A study of the cost of reducing water pollution by a beet sugar factory in the U.S. shows how the cost increases exponentially with the percentage of waste eliminated. Reducing the volume of organic waste by up to 30 per-

cent costs less than $ 2 per kg eliminated; reducing it by over 65 percent more than $ 20 a kg, and with a reduction of 95 percent each kilogram eliminated costs over $ 120. If the ultimate objective were a 'completely clean' operation, the cost would be a hundred times higher than if 30 percent of the waste were eliminated.

2. An estimate of the cost of reducing air pollution in an American city is given in Table 3.9.

The Netherlands Central Planning Bureau studied the financial implications of pollution control (1975). The construction of sewage treatment plants and other facilities needed to keep the problem within reasonable limits would cost $ 3¼ billion (1972 prices). Running costs would be over $ 800 million a year, or 1.5 percent of the national income. Allowing for greater pollution owing to increases in population, the number of motor vehicles, and energy consumption, it is estimated that costs incurred for the environment will rise from 0.3 percent of the national income in 1973 to about 2 percent in 1985.

Table 3.9. Estimated cost of reducing air pollution in an American city

Percentage reduction: Sulphur dioxide (SO_2)	Particulate matter	Estimated cost ($)
5	22	50,000
42	66	750,000
48	69	2,600,000

The study had to leave some forms of pollution out of account for lack of data, including the disposal of radioactive waste, the thermal pollution of surface waters, and noise. Unfortunately, no definition was given of the term 'reasonable limits'.

Conclusions and principles for a model

More and more regional and national organisations are being formed to fight pollution. They include Ministries for the Environment, monitoring authorities, and research institutions. Similar organisations will also have to deal with pollution internationally.

The cost of stopping the worst pollution is mostly estimated at 3 to 4 percent of the gross national income. However, in view of the existing inadequacies in pollution control, the continuing uncertainty about the true situation (natural delays, long-term effects, and so on), and the desire to go on increasing industrial output in developing countries, ultimately bringing it to the level of the rich nations, *the model will assume that 5 percent of the national income is allocated for pollution control. We fully realise that here again there is no guarantee of pollution being kept within acceptable limits. As the building process is comparatively primitive and uses few materials, however, we see no need to include additional limitations on the pollution this sector causes.*

3.6 Sharing prosperity

The usual approach to the question of an equitable prosperity level is to ask what the maximum income of the rich should be. The question can be reversed: what are the minimum needs of the poor, and what should their income then be? In any event they do need a certain minimum of food, medical care, footwear, clothing, and shelter.

At the 1974 U.N. Conference in Bucharest on population problems the poor nations rightly argued that the first requirement for population planning was increased prosperity. Sixty nations, members of the Group of 77, demanded at the U.N. Conference on Trade and Development (UNCTAD, Algiers, 1975) that the developing nations' share of industrial production should increase from 7 percent to 20 – 25 percent between now and the year 2000.

The scope for income transfers within social and economic structures is bound by certain rules. After the Sixth General Assembly of the United Nations a project group was set up under the name 'Reshaping the International Order' (RIO), with J. Tinbergen as the coordinator (1976). To ensure a peaceful world it was considered essential for the inequality in incomes to be reduced to a ratio of 1:3 in the next 40 years. This is roughly the present ratio between poor and rich regions in the European Community, which Tinbergen hardly considers acceptable.

Conclusions and principles for a model

For the future relationship between rich and poor nations we shall aim at an income distribution that is ultimately equal. As regards internal distribution within the individual territories, we shall adopt a distribution in which the rich earn not more than twice as much as the poor.

The implications of equitable income distribution and more economical use of materials are found to be very far-reaching and complex. It is impractical to indicate all the consequences. Besides this, they are not within the scope of this study. We shall nevertheless try to outline some implications.

If there is much greater uniformity in remuneration, no further use can be made of cheap, underpaid labour. The norms and values of labour and remuneration will probably change completely. This will also influence the motivation to study, to seek a career, and so on. Equitable distribution of prosperity will also have to comprise income from profits. The notion of profit will obviously have to be redefined, partly because exponential growth will be slowed down.

We said in Chapter 1 that we shall assume that the requisite organisations exist and that the required measures are put into effect. A necessary consequence of this is that the possession of natural resources should no longer imply international power. A major problem is how and by whom decisions will be taken without involving unacceptable over-planning. The possession of a limited amount of resources will make it necessary to ascertain needs, analyse production processes, and judge where the scarce materials are to be used. Products and production processes will have to be standardised to avoid unnecessary losses and make products last longer. Market processes will have to function within close limits, defined so that the conditions of income distribution and use of resources are satisfied. Within these peripheral conditions, however, it must still be possible to exchange local surpluses at prices determined by the model in order to achieve maximum prosperity.

Table 3.10. Limiting values

Resources	Reserves Known reserves (10⁶ t, 1970)	World production (10⁶ t, 1970)	Sufficient for x years if consumption unchanged	consumption increases	Growth rate (%)	Energy Required energy (kgce/tonne product)	Atmospheric pollution in kg/tonne product Particulate matter	CO	CO₂	HF	SO₂	NOₓ	CₓHᵧ	Consumption 2020 % for housing	Available per housing unit (kg)[a]
Steel	100,000	420	240	93	1.8	1,000	1.6	8.5	+	0.1-0.3	1.7	2.7	+	5	857
Aluminium	1,170	11.7	100	31	6.4	4,200	1-4.5	+	+	0.03-0.6	+	+	+	5	10.1
Copper	308	8.5	36	21	4.6	2,450	+	+	+	+	+	+	+	5	2.6
Lead	91	3.5	26	21	2	1,850	+	+	+	+	+	+	+	5	0.8
Zinc	123	5.4	23	18	2.9	1,850	+	+	+	+	+	+	+	5	1.1
Stone	large	?				1	+								
Sand	large	?				1	+								
Gravel/Chippings	large	?				1	+		+	+	+	+	+		
Lime	large	?				215	0.3-3		600		0.7-1.7	+	+	50	
Cement	large	535				170	0.3-2		500	+	0.5-1.4	+	+	25	
Bricks	large	?				150	0.5				0.4-1.2			75	
Sand-lime bricks	large	?				15	0.5		45		0.1-0.2			50	
Concrete	large	3,100				9	0.1-0.7		170		0.2-0.5			25	
Glass	large	30				700	+		186	+	0.7-1.7	+	+	15	
Plastics	large	30				1,800	+			+	2.3	+	1.5	5	
Timber	120 × 10⁹ m³	2.1 × 10⁹ m³				0.8	+			+	+			20	12 m³ [b]
Coal	5,000,000	2,200	2,300	111	4.1									5	42,857[c]
Mineral oil/petroleum	58,000	1,870	31	20	3.9									5	711[c]
Tar sands	15,000	?	?											5	184[c]
Natural gas	3 × 10¹³ m³	7.9 × 10¹¹ m³	38	22	4.7									5	334[c]

a. Taking the economic life of a housing unit as 50 years, density of occupation 4 persons, world population 7 × 10⁹, consumption 60% of reserves in 100 years.
b. Taking unchanged consumption of 2.1 × 10⁹ m³/year.
c. In kg CE; total for fossil fuels 44,086 kg CE.

4. Basic elements of the building process

4.1 Specific input data

In Chapter 3 we endeavoured to arrive at the principal general input data needed for the model. We are now concerned specifically with building data. Ultimately, limiting values will have to be established for every housing unit with respect to the building materials available, energy, permissible pollution, and so on. Chapter 5 will examine whether the limits are in fact adequate for the complete design of a house.

4.1.1 Energy

The question arises whether it would be possible to express all economic factors in energy units. Particularly in recent years research has been carried out at many places into the energy requirements of a wide range of processes. Plenty of data exist on the energy needed to recover a more usable form of energy from the various sources. In the Netherlands the research is co-ordinated by the National Steering Group for Energy Research (LSEO). International co-ordination is in the hands of the International Federation of Institutes for Advanced Studies (IFIAS). The relationship between energy consumption and economic structure is also being studied. An example concerning the Netherlands is the study by P. J. J. Lesuis and F. Muller (1976).

Examination shows that nearly all studies disregard human labour. If it were possible to convert human labour into energy units, the entire economic process could ultimately be expressed in terms of energy exchange. Human labour, however, is very difficult to convert into a unit. This is because of the many economic, social, cultural, and religious differences between population groups. In a world in which remuneration, energy, and material allocations were all made in the same way, this difficulty could be disposed of to some extent.

The energy analysis for the building process is as follows:
1. determine the energy needed to obtain the natural resources and to make building materials such as bricks, cement, wood, and steel;

2. determine the energy needed to manufacture prefabricated elements such as steel staircases, aluminium window frames, kitchens, and heating;
3. determine the on-site energy needed to put the elements together;
4. the remaining energy consumption is determined by reference to the relationship found to exist between energy consumption and income (see Chapter 6).

4.1.2 Materials

For proper determination of the amount of energy used the quantities of material used must also be known. But this is not easy to analyse. Although the basic materials are fairly easy to ascertain, difficulties arise in the case of prefabricated elements. These have also been studied to ascertain what resources they consume, but where this was impossible, the macro-economic ratios in Chapter 6 were taken.

4.1.3 Work and money

Bearing in mind that about 60 percent of the cost of building a conventional Western home consists of labour, this factor obviously requires careful analysis. The on-site working time can be ascertained exactly; detailed analyses of this already exist. Jelsma (1973), for instance, has given the times for all the work on foundations, bricklaying, pointing and plastering, carpentry, and so on.

The difficulties we encountered in the material analysis exist with regard to labour as well. Owing to lack of information, some factors had to be left out. They include transport from factory to site and the use of equipment such as cranes and concrete mixers. The time needed for manufacturing conventional and prefabricated elements is difficult to ascertain. All these factors could only be expressed in terms of money. Consequently, we decided to include the aggregate cost of the house as a limitation in addition to the limiting values for materials and energy. One of the points of departure in Chapter 1 was a redistribution of prosperity. This will also influence the amount expendable per housing unit. The reference currency is the standard 1970 dollar.

4.1.4 The technical life of a house

In order to decide the number of housing units to be built each year, their useful life must be known. The literature gives two ways of calculating this, both leading to about the same result.

The Netherlands Central Bureau of Statistics uses a method based on the stock of existing houses at a given moment. The number of years taken to build up this stock is calculated from statistical data; from these follows the average useful life, on the assumption that the oldest houses will be pulled down first. In actual fact, there will be some variation. But this is of little importance to the result of the calculations: for every house with a longer than average life there is also one with a shorter life. The average life arrived at in this way is 110 years (see Appendix B).

Another method is that of L. Tas (1969). His starting point is the age structure of the stock of houses and the mortality rate per age group, precisely the same as the usual demographic method of calculating the death rate. The mortality rate for a given group is the quotient of the number of withdrawals and the opening stock in a given period. Data are available for a number of years on the age of houses taken out of stock. From these, the mortality rate can be calculated for a given age group. By this method, the average life is found to be 108 years.

The results of the above calculations are only approximations since there is a dearth of reliable statistics, particularly for houses built before 1920. They are also subject to change. This is clear, for instance, from the method applied by the Central Bureau of Statistics twenty years ago, which indicated an average life 10 years longer than at present. The outcome is also influenced by a number of technical, economic, and social factors, such as the nature of the materials used, the degree of city-forming, and housing standards.

4.1.5   The economic life of a house

During their 110 years' average life, houses will be altered or renovated to varying degrees. They also have to be repaired and maintained during this time. The cost of this and of the materials cannot be disregarded in this study. It was examined how much the average annual repair and maintenance costs are and what renovations and minor alterations are made during the life of a house.

Figures for this were obtained from a number of renovation projects of the Dutch National Housing Council (1973). The figures are those of several large housing associations, which can be taken as representative. The norms for repair, maintenance, and renovation differ considerably from place to place and from time to time. The figure found for economic life will therefore have to be regarded as an approximation.

For a number of houses of very different ages repair and maintenance was found to cost $ 75 a year (1972). In 1972 dollars these houses cost on average some $ 16,500 to build. Repair and maintenance during the entire technical life of the house (110 × $ 75) is therefore half the original cost, or 0.5 x.

The reports also showed that a house usually undergoes major alterations (renovation) 50 years after being built. This costs an average of $ 100 per sq.m, whereas new building would cost $ 200. The cost of renovation is therefore equal to 0.5 x.

Routine repair and maintenance can therefore be combined for convenience into two 25-yearly renovations, 25 and 75 years respectively after building, at an estimated cost of 0.125 x per minor alteration.

The sum of building costs, annual repair and maintenance, renovation, and minor alterations is 2.25 times the cost of building. The economic life is now arrived at by dividing the technical life by 2.25.

In view of the lack of accuracy in the figures, this can be rounded off to 50 years.

4.2 A static approach to the limiting values

Table 3.10 listed a number of factors for examination. It relates present known reserves to the time within which they will be exhausted if consumption remains unchanged and also if it increases. The principal sources were the First Report of the Club of Rome (1972), P. C. Kreyger (1974), M. K. Hubbert (1968), The World Power Conference (1968), and *The Oil and Gas Journal* (1972).

The table also shows the energy needed to make 1,000 kg product of certain building materials. It also indicates the consequent atmospheric pollution caused by particulate matter – carbon monoxide (CO), carbon dioxide (CO_2), hydrogen fluoride (HF), sulphur dioxide (SO_2), nitrogen oxides (NO_x) and hydrocarbons (C_xH_y).

Lastly, an initial, static approach to the problems of distribution was attempted. In the first instance, the percentage of the main building materials intended for housing was determined. It was next calculated how much can be made available per house in the year 2020 on the following basis:

Economic life of house:	50 years
Density of occupation:	4 persons
Consumption of resources:	40% of 1970 known reserves in 50 years
World population:	7 billion

In this way a list of limiting values is obtained which gives an initial indication of the limits within which consumption for housing purposes may have to be kept. This rough, static approximation has the advantage, that, together with the results of the test cases in Chapter 5, it can be seen fairly quickly what kinds of houses are still practicable within the given limits.

It must, of course, be borne in mind that the existing data are probably too rough and too localised for use as absolute limiting values. If we want a useful and reliable world model, it will have to include remuneration of labour, and also an amount of money as a limit upon factors not already expressed in the limits on materials, energy, and pollution.

In addition, allowance must be made for the interrelationship and interaction between the various factors. For this purpose a dynamic simulation model was devised to make these refinements. It is discussed in Chapter 6.

Conclusions and principles for a model

Recapitulating, the following values relating specifically to housing will be introduced into the model:

1. *For every house the consumption of materials and energy must remain within specific limits; where it was not possible to establish directly the consumption of energy and materials, the macro-economic correlation found to exist with income was used;*
2. *In view of the use of labour, a limitation was also set for the overall cost of a house, which must be observed in the design;*
3. *The economic life of a house can be taken as 50 years.*

The factors determining the average occupancy of a house, the number of houses to be built, and a building worker's hourly pay are discussed in Chapter 6.

5. Possibilities for quantitative analysis of housing: test cases

5.1 The purpose of the test cases

Before the principles worked out in the previous chapters can be put into practice, they must first be tried out under realistic conditions. Such test cases are all the more important because they provide the necessary information about the requirements which a dynamic housing model must satisfy if its results are to serve as guidelines in design.

The test cases were chosen so that information is obtained about various levels of development; we studied:
1. a simple house on wooden posts in Surinam;
2. a house developed in the West for development countries, in this case Ghana;
3. a largely prefabricated house in the wealthy countries.

Each design was analysed with respect to the following basic aspects:
1. material consumption;
2. the energy used in manufacturing the materials and, if possible, that needed for making the prefabricated parts, for building, and for transport to the site;
3. the labour used in building;
4. the aggregate building costs.

The results for each test case are summarised below.

5.2 Carib home in Surinam

Caribs are Indians inhabiting the lower reaches of the Marowijne, the river forming the boundary between Surinam and French Guyana. They live mainly by fishing, farming, and hunting. The villages are inhabited by several hundred people; they have a simple structure and the settlement pattern is uniform. Building is entirely on traditional lines. The first house is usually

built almost without anyone else's help, because a man has to prove his worth.
At first this house is small, but more space is needed when children are born. If
a bigger house is built, then a brother, brother-in-law, or other relative will
usually be asked to help.

Kloos (1972) gives a full description of these Carib homes. They are built in
groups, separated by bushes and small gardens. They are of very simple
design (Figure 5.1).

Figure 5.1. Pile-dwelling in Surinam (perspective drawing)

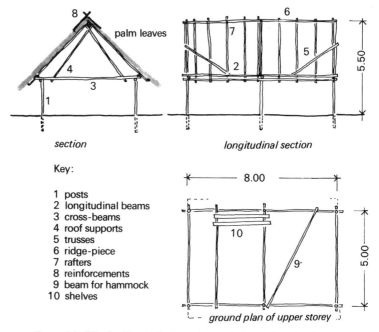

Key:

1 posts
2 longitudinal beams
3 cross-beams
4 roof supports
5 trusses
6 ridge-piece
7 rafters
8 reinforcements
9 beam for hammock
10 shelves

Figure 5.2. Pile-dwelling in Surinam (ground plan and sections)

A Carib house is usually little more than a palm-leaf roof on six or eight posts. Some have palm-leaf walls. Other people often help to fell the supporting beams, to fetch and lay the roof covering. One house provides accommodation for an average of five or six persons (see Figure 5.2).

Many families have more than one house. A smaller one is often built next to the first to function as a kitchen. If a new home is built, the old one is often kept on as a workplace or shed. Our calculations were based on a family averaging 5 to 6 people, together having $1\frac{1}{2}$ houses.

Constructional features

After a suitable location has been chosen, the site is prepared. The trees required for construction are felled, stripped of their leaves, and brought to the site. Next the holes in which the posts are placed are dug. When the holes are filled in and the posts notched, the frame is put in position. Next the longitudinal beams can be fixed. The three frames are made on the ground, set up, and fixed with temporary struts. These are next replaced by permanent trusses, after which the ridge-piece is fitted. It is now time to start felling, stripping, and fetching the rafters. In the meantime the palm leaves, split and tied together, are first left to dry for some weeks. In the forest liana is collected for fixing the leaves to the rafters. Then the leaves for the roof covering can be put on. These eventually form a thick, waterproof cover. Lastly the ridge is reinforced with heavy branches fixed together.

As neither the timber nor the palm leaves are preserved, the life of the house is only seven years.

Materials

The detailed study by Kloos (1972) shows that construction requires 47 trees. For the roof covering as many as 65 trees are felled, and there is no further use for the trunks. This makes a total of 112 trees for one house per family. As stated above, each family has an average of $1\frac{1}{2}$ houses. This makes 168 trees per family. Taking a tree as 5 metres long with a mean diameter of 10 cm, this is 6.6 cu.m timber. It can also be assumed that an average of 10 kg iron is used in nails, etc.

Energy

The materials can be converted into energy with Table 3.9. The timber corresponds to 2.64 kg CE, and the iron represents 10 kg CE. The total energy consumption is thus 12.64 CE.

Labour

Kloos arrives at the following estimate of the labour required per house:

	man-days
Building and construction	20
Transport and fixing roof covering	15
Total	35

Related to a normal Western 8-hour working day, this means that 420 man-hours are needed for $1\frac{1}{2}$ houses.

Conclusions

As noted above, the life of a Carib house is only seven years. In order to make the test cases comparable, the economic life of 50 years calculated in Chapter 4 was taken as a basis. For the Carib house, therefore, the figures will have to be multiplied by 7. This gives the following comparison:

		7 years	50 years
Materials:	timber	168 trees (6.6 cu.m)	1,176 trees (46 cu.m)
	iron	10 kg	70 kg
Energy		12.64 kg CE	88 kg CE
Labour		420 man-hours	2,940 man-hours

The living area is 40 sq.m + 25 sq.m (upper storey) = 65 sq.m per house; for $1\frac{1}{2}$ houses it is 97 sq.m. Number of occupants 5 to 6.

If the labour is valued at $ 4 an hour, which is comparable with the wage level given by the simulation model for the poor nations in the year 2020 (see Chapter 6), this represents for 50 years:

Wages		2,940 man-hours at $ 4	= $ 11,760
Materials:	timber	46 cu.m at $ 40	= $ 1,840
	iron		= $ 280
Total building cost			$ 13,880

5.3 Living in developing countries: Ghana development plan

Owing to the construction of the Barikese Dam in Ghana, an entire village had to be moved. Under the auspices of the International Course on Housing, Building, and Planning at the Bouwcentrum, Rotterdam, a number of prototypes for better homes were designed.

Ingenious and thoroughly researched designs were developed, based largely on simple methods appropriate to local facilities and materials, with the exception of the corrugated aluminium roofs. They included a detailed work schedule indicating the time for each operation. Wages were taken at only $ 0.85 a day. Family ties are very close in Ghana, and in rural areas whole families often live together; the house is therefore occupied by 12 to 19 persons. The Ghana house is as shown in Figure 5.3.

Constructional features

The structure of the house is roughly as follows. The foundation beams and floors are made of concrete. Walls are built of sand-lime blocks. The whole is strengthened with a reinforced concrete beam poured all round on the outside walls, on which the roof structure is fixed. Roofing consists of corrugated aluminium sheets. Doors, window frames, and ceilings are made of wood.

Materials

Sand (foundations and walls)	131.5 tonnes
Gravel (ditto)	46.9 tonnes
Cement (ditto)	18.8 tonnes
Steel (concrete-beam reinforcement)	0.36 tonnes
Aluminium (roofing)	0.44 tonnes
Glass (window panes)	0.24 tonnes
Wood (window frames, doors, and roof)	3.5 cu.m

The table does not include materials needed for sanitary fittings, drains, or electrical installation.

Energy

The energy embodied in the materials was calculated by converting them with the energy factors in Table 3.9:

Sand	131.5×1.1	144.65 kg CE
Gravel	46.9×1.1	51.59 kg CE
Cement	18.83×170	3,200.59 kg CE
Steel	$0.356 \times 1,000$	356.0 kg CE
Aluminium	$0.44 \times 4,200$	1,848.0 kg CE
Glass	0.24×700	168.0 kg CE
Wood	3.5×0.4	1.4 kg CE
Total energy consumption		5,770.23 kg CE

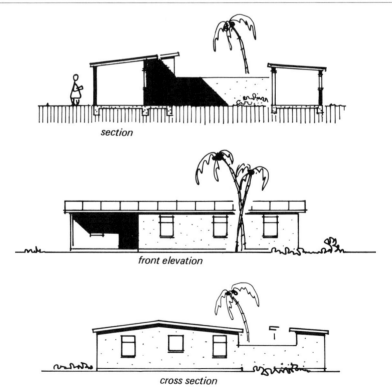

section

front elevation

cross section

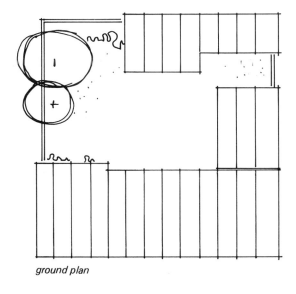

ground plan

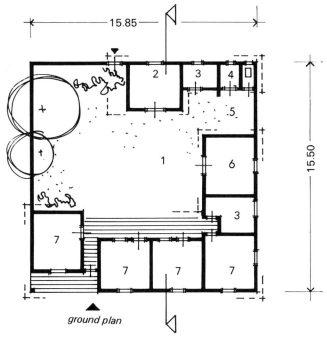

ground plan

Figure 5.3. Plan of a house in Ghana: 1. patio, 2. kitchen, 3. storage space, 4. bath, 5. wash room, 6. living accommodation, 7. bedrooms.

The energy needed for manufacturing the aluminium roofing sheets could not be ascertained; energy used in building is not included.

Labour

The estimates showed that building required a total of 2,588 man-hours. The homes are comparatively cheap to build, solely because of the low wage averaging $ 0.85 a day.

Conclusions

Having regard to the materials and building method, the economic life of the house can be taken as 50 years (see Chapter 4). In order to compare the houses in the different test cases, the figures were converted to 5 or 6 occupants:

	12 to 19 occupants	5 to 6 occupants
Materials:		
sand	131.50 tonnes	43.80 tonnes
gravel	46.90 tonnes	15.60 tonnes
cement	18.83 tonnes	6.28 tonnes
steel	0.36 tonnes	0.12 tonnes
aluminium	0.44 tonnes	0.15 tonnes
glass	0.24 tonnes	0.08 tonnes
wood	3.50 m³	1.17 m³
Total energy	5,770.23 kg CE	1,923.40 kg CE
Labour	2,588 man-hours	862.70 man-hours
Living area	120 sq.m	40 sq.m

Taking labour at $ 4 an hour as in the first test case, this gives for 50 years with 5 to 6 occupants:

Wages	863 man-hours at $ 4	$ 3,452
Materials		$ 807
Total building cost		$ 4,259

This does not include the cost of sanitary fittings, drains, or electrical installation.

5.4 Living in the industrial society

The third type of house analysed was the type of terraced house often seen in recent new housing developments in the Netherlands (Figure 5.4).

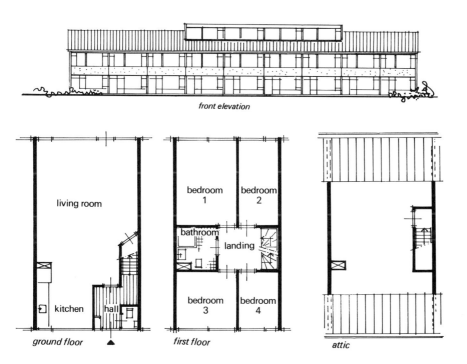

Figure 5.4. A Western, semi-prefabricated house

Constructional features

These houses are semi-prefabricated. Walls and floors are factory-made, transported to the site, and joined together with concrete. They are finished by traditional methods. End walls and dividing walls are built by hand. Back and front outside walls are largely built up of wooden door and window frames, often timbered.

The very detailed estimates available made possible a precise analysis of these houses. The following materials, energy, and labour relate to a family of 5 to 6 persons:

Materials

Concrete (footing, floors and walls)	36 cu.m
Lime/gypsum (plastering)	3.97 tonnes
Steel (concrete reinforcement)	3.26 tonnes
Aluminium (sections)	0.05 tonnes
Window glass	0.54 tonnes
Bricks (masonry, 4,345 bricks)	8.56 tonnes
Wood (door and window frames, beams)	7.5 cu.m.
Plastics (piping and conduits)	0.1 tonnes
Lead (flashings)	0.03 tonnes
Copper (piping)	0.06 tonnes

This includes the central heating installation, drains, plumbing, and sanitary fittings, but not the electrical installation.

Energy

Concrete	36×60	2,160	kg CE
Lime/gypsum	3.97×215	853.55	kg CE
Steel	$3.262 \times 1,000$	3,262	kg CE
Aluminium	$0.05 \times 4,200$	210	kg CE
Glass	0.54×700	378	kg CE
Bricks	8.558×150	1,283.7	kg CE
Wood	8.44×0.8	6.75	kg CE
Plastics	$0.1 \times 1,800$	180	kg CE
Lead	$0.026 \times 1,843$	47.92	kg CE
Copper	$0.061 \times 2,457$	149.88	kg CE
Total energy		8,531.8	kg CE

In reality, more energy is used, because that needed for producing the prefabricated elements could not be ascertained; energy used in building is not included either.

Labour

On-site man-hours 560; this does not include production of prefabricated elements.

Conclusions

As shown in Chapter 4, the economic life of the house can be put at 50 years. As on average 5 to 6 persons live in such a house, the figures need no further conversion. The floor area is 120 sq.m. Taking labour costs at $ 5 an hour (comparable with the simulation model for the wealthy nations in the year 2020), the cost of a house is:

Labour 560 × $ 5	$ 2,800
Materials	$ 11,153
Total cost	$ 13,953

5.5 Comparison of test cases

Kloos (1972) gives a number of reasons why the social structure of a Caribbean community and the material form of the home can become harmonised. In the first place, the material form itself is simple and unspecialised. Nor is its life longer than seven years. After this, the occupant largely has to renovate the house and adapt it to new circumstances or viewpoints. Indeed, every occupant is his own principal, architect, and contractor. Many writers (Arendt, 1959; Alexander, 1964; Jones, 1970; and Foqué, 1975) have pointed out the importance of close relations between the parties concerned in the building process.

The gap between designer and occupant is already greater in the case of the house in Ghana. Since the local population is enlisted in the building process (self-help housing), however, there is still a degree of involvement.

In Dutch terraced houses there is hardly ever any direct relationship between the architect and the (anonymous) occupant, while the occupant plays no part at all in the building process.

Table 5.1. Comparison of test cases

Test case	Floor area	Cost of materials	Energy	Man-hours	Total cost
Surinam	97 sq.m	$ 2,222	88 kg CE	2,940	$ 14,444
Ghana	40 sq.m	$ 833	1,923 kg CE	860	$ 4,400
Netherlands	120 sq.m	$ 11,000	8,500 kg CE	560	$ 13,500

If the figures from the three test cases are compared on the basis of:
– average economic life 50 years;
– average occupancy 5 to 6 persons;
– hourly wage $ 4,
the comparison given in Table 5.1 is obtained.
Figure 5.5 gives a relative comparison of the test cases.

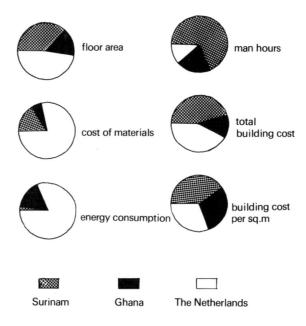

Figure 5.5. Relative comparison of the test cases.

The Surinam home is relatively expensive because of the high timber consumption and the high labour factor. On the other hand, energy consumption
is very low indeed. The cost of materials for the Ghana house is comparatively
low. The use of the aluminium roof makes energy consumption fairly high.
Compared with the other two types of houses, the covered living area is small.
The Dutch house has a big floor surface, high material costs, and high energy
consumption. The number of on-site man-hours is low. It must be borne in
mind, however, that the man-hours involved in the production of inter-
mediate products are not included.

Comparison of cost per sq.m floor surface is remarkable: Surinam $ 148 per
sq.m, the Netherlands $ 112, and Ghana $ 110. If Surinam incomes were

redistributed and wages raised to the Dutch level, the Surinam house would be dearer per sq.m than the Dutch house. This is because of the primitive building methods and the house's short life.

This recalls the old saying that quality pays. Apart from this, the high timber consumption would hardly be justified on a large scale. The choice of production methods is, of course, greatly influenced by wage levels. The high cost of the house in Ghana is largely attributable to the hand-making of sand-cement blocks.

Conclusions

The building process can be sufficiently quantified to ascertain the use of labour, materials, and energy. This means that enough input data are now available to design houses with the results of the model. But a number of factors will have to be expressed in monetary terms, as the analysis of the semi-prefabricated house in the Netherlands has clearly shown.

6. The simulation model

6.1 General scheme of the model

As we have seen in Chapter 2, a simulation model can describe the quantitative relation between a number of factors. The principal factors included in the model are population, income, income distribution, food supplies, pollution, materials, and housing. Figure 6.1 gives a simplified diagram of the various relationships and variables occurring in the model.

The model makes a distinction between poor and rich nations. Income distribution between the two should satisfy the conditions of Chapter 3. The use of scarce resources and energy is found to be related directly to income. Lastly, the building sector is included in the model in detail, because the model must indicate the amounts of scarce resources and energy made available for building or renovating houses.

The previous chapters have already given many model input data. Taking the basic values for 1970 and the existing interrelationships, it is possible to ascertain how the variables develop in the course of time. Figure 6.2 shows the trend in a number of major variables. Population and income are still found to grow vigorously at first. After some time, however, growth slackens off. The birth control measures assumed in the model then begin to take effect. As more and more investment is needed for exploiting resources, the growth in income also slows down.

The results of the model are greatly influenced by the time limit within which the objectives have to be attained. It will take at least forty years for the population to stabilise. It also takes a considerable time before the results of income transfers become evident. Another factor is the economic life of the house, which can be put at 50 years. Lastly, there is a psychological argument. If a pattern of the future is to be outlined which is acceptable to everyone concerned, its results must be within reach of the people themselves, or in any case of their children. Fifty years thus seems the most suitable time for a model to cover. The starting point was taken as 1970, because this was the year for which the most recent statistics were available.

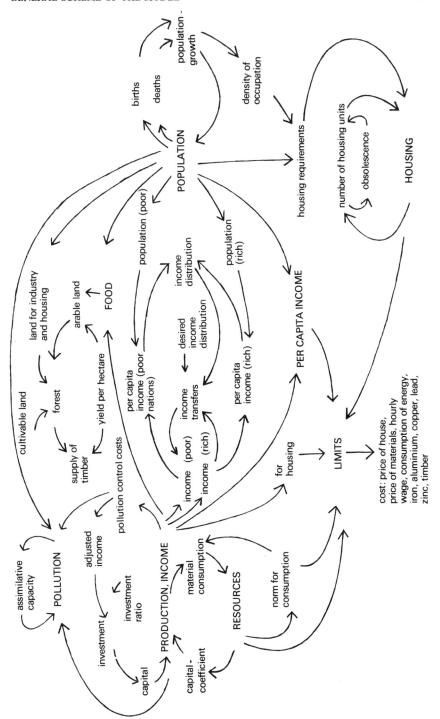

Figure 6.1. Flow-diagram showing major relationships

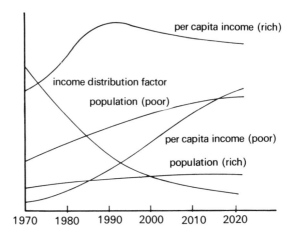

Figure 6.2. Trend in some major factors

6.2 Income trends

An important factor determining income is the stock of capital goods, consisting of plant and machinery, transport, etc. This stock is the result of cumulative investment over a period of time. Production does not consist solely of consumer goods, but part is reserved for capital goods (the investment ratio). As the stock of capital goods increases, production increases as well. The ratio between production and the capital it requires is known as the capital coefficient.

Statistics on the proportion of gross domestic product that is invested are given in the *U.N. statistical yearbook*. The wealthy nations' investment ratio is higher than the poor nations' (average 23 percent against 15 percent) but probably decreases again with very high incomes (in the United States, for instance, it is 17 percent). Against this, the poor nations' capital coefficient is slightly higher. In view of the shortage of capital, these countries probably concentrate on sectors requiring comparatively little capital.

The capital coefficient can be calculated as follows:

$$\frac{1}{k} = \frac{\dot{y}}{s} \; ,$$

in which $\frac{1}{k}$ is the productivity of capital (the converse of capital output

ratio k), y is the relative increase in gross domestic product, and s the investment ratio.

Statistics on the growth of the gross domestic product are to be found in the
U.N. statistical yearbook. The poor nations' capital coefficient is found to
average 3.2 and the rich nations' 4.1. Disregarding income transfers, the rich
nations' growth will therefore be somewhat greater than the poor nations'
(5.8 compared with 4.8 percent). But bearing in mind that the disparities are in
fact reduced by these very income transfers, the calculations can be based on
an average investment ratio of 20 percent and an average capital coefficient of
4, giving a growth in gross domestic product of 5 percent per annum. The
national disposable income is then arrived at by adding the balance of primary and secondary income transfers to the gross domestic product.
    One should realise that transfers of income are not financial transactions
alone but that they also have day-to-day implications. A country with an
income-transfer surplus will consume part of the income directly, for instance
by buying food abroad. The remainder can then be applied in increasing the
stock of capital goods (by importing machinery and means of transport). In
turn, these capital goods contribute to future production. In this way a cumulative process of development is initiated. The reverse applies to the rich
nations, where there is a relative lag in capital formation because of the
transfers of income.

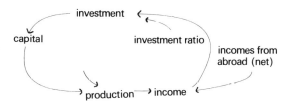

Figure 6.3. Income formation

Although the rich nations' income growth is greatly slowed down by this,
their average per capita income remains at the 1970 level.
    It is assumed that the same percentage of income transfers as of the gross
domestic product is expended on capital goods, and the investment ratio can
then be expressed as a percentage of disposable national income.
    The relationships governing income formation are shown in Figure 6.3.
    Another adverse effect on income growth is caused through basic materials

becoming dearer and dearer. The scarcer they become, the more increasingly inaccessible reserves have to be opened up, and the more expensive they get. This means that the capital coefficient increases as well, slowing down income growth. The increase in capital costs is already evident in oil exploration and recovery. This negative feedback loop is shown in Figure 6.4.

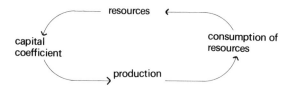

Figure 6.4. Relationship between consumption of resources and capital coefficient

The relationship between depletion of natural resources and capital require-ments was studied by D.L. Meadows and W. W. Behrens (1974); this is the source of the graph in Figure 6.5.

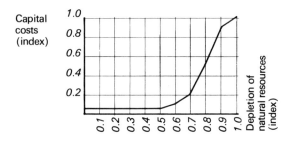

Figure 6.5. Depletion of natural resources and capital costs

6.3 Income distribution

The World Bank publishes estimates of per capita incomes in the World Bank Atlas. Comparison shows a clear dividing line at a (1970) per capita income of $ 600, apparently the boundary between rich and poor. The great majority of nations had an average per capita income of less than $ 600. It is probably very difficult to break through this barrier.

The criterion adopted for the inequity of income distribution was the ratio between the rich nations' average income compared with the poor nations.' While the rich nations' average income in 1970 was $ 2,360 (comparable with that in the Netherlands or the United Kingdom), a poor nation had to be content with an average of $ 169 (comparable with nations like Kenya and China). Inhabitants of the rich countries in 1970 therefore earned on average fourteen times as much as inhabitants of the poor countries. If the great disparities in the countries themselves are taken into account, obviously many people are really in a far worse position.

As set out in Chapter 3, the model will be based on an income distribution that will ultimately be the same. The income inequality factor, which was still 14 in 1970, is gradually decreased. The targets are a factor of 3 by 1980, 2 by 1985, 1.5 by 1995, and 1 by 2020. Each year this desirable distribution is then compared with the true distribution. Some time is needed to adapt the trend to the desired situation. A period of fifteen years would seem a reasonable assumption for this. In this way there will always be a lag in actual income distribution compared with the desirable distribution, but it will be picked up fairly quickly. The mechanism determining income transfers is shown in Figure 6.6. The result of this process is that the income inequality factor is reduced to 1.45 by the year 2020.

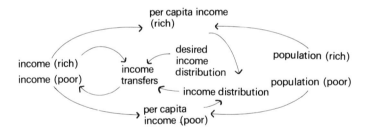

Figure 6.6. The mechanism of income transfers

The poor nations' per capita income is then $ 2,166 and the rich nations' $ 3,157. The poor will then have almost reached the Netherlands' 1970 level, while the rich nations' incomes increase on average to a level comparable with France or Germany, but considerably less than the United States and Canada already had in 1970.

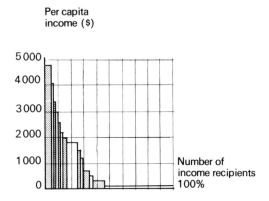

Figure 6.7. Income distribution in 1970

Figure 6.7 illustrates the inequity of world income distribution in 1970, while Figure 6.8 shows the situation in the year 2020, if the results of our model should be achieved.

One may wonder whether the income transfers needed to reach this objective are not inordinately high; but this is not really so bad. Though the required amounts are substantial in absolute terms (a maximum of $ 213 billion in 1995), they are fairly modest when related to income: not more than 3.5 percent of the rich nations' income is required to raise the poor nations ultimately to the same level of development.

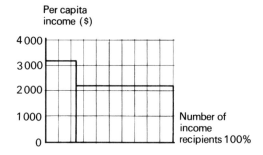

Figure 6.8. Income distribution in 2020

In order to ascertain the per capita growth in income an adjustment must be made for population growth; this is dealt with below.

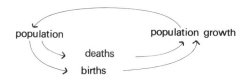

Figure 6.9. Population growth

6.4 Population

The factors determining population growth have been discussed in Chapter 3. The increase in the population is related to the birth and death rates. This feed-back mechanism is shown in Figure 6.9.

The model assumes that a drop in the birth rate will ensure that population growth will stop by the year 2020. The birth rate and the death rate should then be in equilibrium.

In 1970 there were 2.48 billion poor people and 1.19 billion rich people, on the basis of our boundary line of $ 600 per capita. As population growth in the poor nations is greater than in the rich ones, however, the (formerly) poor nations will have a population of 5.35 billion and the rich nations 1.78 billion in the year 2020. Although the number of poor people increases more than the number of rich, therefore, income transfers ensure that income *disparities* decrease. The poor thus become proportionately less poor. Moreover, the poor by definition become rich once they pass the $ 600 mark. But it is more convenient to go on speaking of rich and poor.

6.5 Housing requirements

The number of housing units that have to be built depends on population, average density of occupation, and the unit's useful life.

As 6.4 has shown, the population will increase by over 3 billion between 1970 and 2020, 2.5 billion of them poor and 0.5 billion rich. We have also seen in Chapter 4 that the economic life of a house can be taken as 50 years. After this time, therefore, a house must either be replaced or renovated.

As for average occupancy per house, this should obviously be linked to population growth and the consequent family structure. Undoubtedly there are also local customs, traditions, and religious views which play a part. Nevertheless, a definite relationship was established between average occupancy and population growth. Comparison of figures for 91 countries shows this relationship to be as follows:

$$Y = \quad 0.73\,X + 2.96 \qquad \text{correlation coefficient } R^2 = 0.53$$
$$\quad\quad (0.07) \quad\quad (0.17) \qquad \text{number of observations } N = 91$$

in which Y is the average rate of occupation;
           X is the average population growth for the past 10 years;
           $(\ldots)$ is the standard error of the regression coefficient.

Although for these reasons the correlation coefficient is not so great ($R^2 =$ 0.53), the standard errors indicate that the regression coefficients are reliable.

The constant term of 2.96 means that with a stable population ($X = 0$) average occupancy per house will still be three persons. Average density of occupation in poor countries would decrease from 5.3 in 1970 to 3.7 in 2020, and in rich countries from 4.5 to 3.6. The ratios are shown in Figure 6.10.

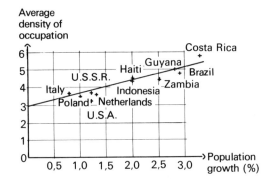

Figure 6.10. Average density of occupation and population growth

Despite the limitation of population growth, the building programme based on the results of the model is still tremendous: 1.5×10^9 houses will have to be built or renovated in the poor countries and 0.5×10^9 in the rich countries.

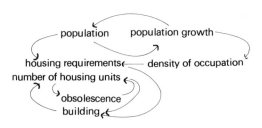

Figure 6.11. Housing requirements

These figures are comparable with the results obtained by J. van Ettinger (1967), who finds a total of 1.1 × 10⁹ units for the period 1958-2000. The mechanism of housing is shown in Figure 6.11.

The model also allows for a certain time-lag between the date a project can be launched and the date by which it is completed.

6.6 Agriculture and forestry

Unlike other natural resources, timber is replenished from year to year. Chapter 3 showed that timber growth can be put at 7 cu.m per hectare per annum. Exploitable forest was conservatively estimated at 2×10^9 hectares, making the potential supply of timber 14×10^9 cu.m.

Every year part of the forests is taken over for other purposes: agriculture, industry, and housing. The land needed for housing and industry is related to the size of the population, while farmland depends on food requirements and yield per hectare. Chapter 1 indicated the hazards associated with chemical fertilisers. The average production per hectare has therefore been kept constant at the 1970 level. The (economic) demand for food is governed by the percentage of income normally spent on this. See Figure 6.12.

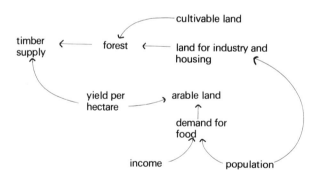

Figure 6.12. The use of land

6.7 Pollution

Pollution is related to population and production. It can be partly eliminated by nature's assimilative capacity. But additional measures are required to control it. Chapter 3 assumed that 5 percent of income will be spent on this. The income after adjustment for this cost will then be available for investment, consumption, and so forth. The various relationships are shown in Figure 6.13.

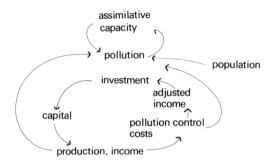

Figure 6.13. Pollution

6.8 The use of scarce resources

As regards the factors determining the consumption of natural resources, a connection was sought with trends in income, population, per capita income, and so on. With these in mind, data were collected for the year 1970 for a large number of countries, the principal sources being the *U.N. statistical yearbook* and *Metal statistics* (*Metallgesellschaft*, Frankfurt a.M.). With the aid of regression analysis, factors were determined which best accounted for the consumption of materials. In all cases national income proved to be the best indicator of basic material consumption. It is disquieting to see that in high per capita income nations there is no falling off in consumption, but that there too consumption is accounted for in the same way. Indeed, nations at a low level of development often had a low consumption of natural resources. In part this has statistical reasons. Less developed nations do not process the materials themselves; these are exported and re-imported after processing. These countries would therefore fit into these ratios better if the basic material content of imports were included. The reverse would apply to the rich nations. It was not possible to examine this hypothesis any further.

The ratios thus found can then be used to assess future demand for natural resources, which is not necessarily the same as the output of mining operations, inasmuch as:

1. part of the final consumption can be met by recycling;
2. there are losses in refining crude materials;
3. there is a slight difference between estimated demand and actual consumption in 1970.

To allow for these, an adjustment was made to bring the figures exactly into line with the output of mining operations in the year 1970. This means, in fact, that the relative volume of recycling, refinery losses, and statistical divergencies is assumed to be constant.

Lastly, allowance should be made for possible economies in consumption.

6.8.1 Energy

Chapter 3 showed that electricity generation from fossil fuels involves considerable losses. Nuclear energy, geothermal energy, and hydro-electric power, however, produce energy more directly. To make the comparison clearer, energy not obtained from fossil fuels has been converted into thermal units (1 kWh el = 3 kWh th).

Investigation of the relevant factors showed that energy consumption is closely related to national income:

$$Y = 2.11 X \qquad \text{correlation coefficient } R^2 = 0.85$$
$$(0.07) \qquad \text{number of observations } N = 54$$

in which Y is the energy consumption (kg CE per capita)
          X is the income ($ per capita).

This relationship is shown in Figure 6.14.

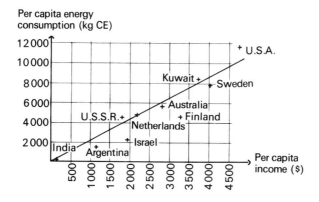

Figure 6.14. Energy consumption and income

The Netherlands is exactly on the regression line: energy consumption is at the level one would expect from the national income. Countries that use a relatively large amount of energy are most of the communist countries and Canada, Norway, Venezuela, and the United States. Consumption is relatively low in Brazil, Denmark, Egypt, France, the German Federal Republic, Greece, Israel, Italy, Switzerland, and Japan.

As regards future energy requirements, it has been assumed that the proportion of non-fossil fuels will remain unchanged (at 7 percent as in 1970).

6.8.2 Iron

Iron consumption is also related to income:

$$Y = 160.5\, X \qquad\qquad R^2 = 0.88$$
$$(5.6) \qquad\qquad\qquad N = 103$$

in which Y is the iron consumption (1,000 tonnes)
$\quad\quad\quad X$ the income (10^9 \$).

The relationship is shown in Figure 6.15.

Consumption above normal is found primarily in the United Kingdom, Italy, and Japan. It is lower than normal in Argentina, India, Pakistan, and the U.S. In the Netherlands it is in line with income.

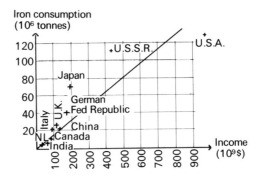

Figure 6.15. Iron consumption and income

6.8.3 Lead

Relationship between lead consumption and income:

$$Y = 0.99\, X \qquad\qquad R^2 = 0.94$$
$$(0.05) \qquad\qquad\quad N = 22$$

in which Y is the lead consumption (1,000 tonnes)
          X is the income (10^9 \$).
   This is depicted in Figure 6.16.

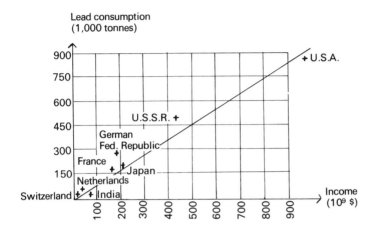

Figure 6.16. Lead consumption and income

Most European countries (including the Netherlands) have a comparatively
high lead consumption, while the U.S., Canada, and India use less than might
be expected on the basis of income.

6.8.4   Zinc

Relationship between zinc consumption and income:

$$Y = 1.30\ X \qquad\qquad\qquad R^2 = 0.89$$
$$(0.08) \qquad\qquad\qquad\qquad N = 23$$

in which Y is the zinc consumption (1,000 tonnes)
          X is the income (10^9 \$).
   This is depicted in Figure 6.17.

Countries with a relatively high consumption are most European countries
(except the Netherlands) and Japan. Consumption is relatively low in the U.S.

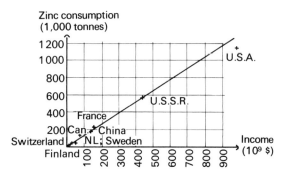

Figure 6.17. Zinc consumption and income

6.8.5 Copper

Relationship between copper consumption and income:

$$Y = 2.07\,X \qquad\qquad\qquad R^2 = 0.93$$
$$(0.11) \qquad\qquad\qquad\qquad N = 21$$

in which Y is the copper consumption (1,000 tonnes)
           X is the income (10^9 $).

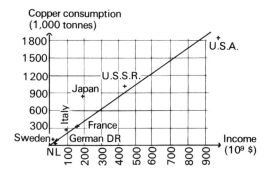

Figure 6.18. Copper consumption and income

Consumption is relatively high in the German Federal Republic and Japan, and relatively low in India, Norway, the U.S., and the Netherlands. This is depicted in Figure 6.18.

6.8.6 Aluminium

Aluminium consumption is also closely related to income:

$$Y = 3.79\,X \qquad\qquad R^2 = 0.98$$
$$(0.11) \qquad\qquad\qquad N = 23$$

in which Y is the aluminium consumption (1,000 tonnes)

            X is the income (10^9 \$).

    Particularly in Japan, and to a less extent in the U.S., more aluminium is used than would be expected from the income, while Canada, China, France, Italy, the U.K., the Soviet Union, and the Netherlands use less. The relationship is shown in Figure 6.19.

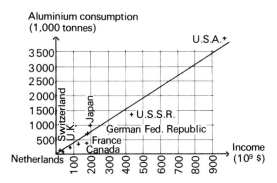

Figure 6.19. Aluminium consumption and income

6.8.7 Timber

It was shown in 6.6 that the potential production of timber is 14×10^9 cu.m. If this is compared with the annual consumption of 2×10^9 cu.m in 1970, there appears to be plenty of timber available for the time being. In addition, over 40 percent of felled timber is at present used for fuel. If the poor nations' level of development rises, it can be assumed that most of this will be superseded by fossil fuels.

    The consumption of timber can be calculated from statistics published annually in the *F.A.O. yearbook of forest products*. Timber not used as fuel is related to income as follows:

$$Y = 0.36\,X \qquad\qquad R^2 = 0.81$$
$$(0.01) \qquad\qquad\qquad N = 145$$

in which Y is the timber consumption (excluding fuel) (10^6 cu.m)
         X the income (10^9 $).
    The relationship is depicted in Figure 6.20.
    Consumption is relatively low in the U.S., India, the U.K., the German
Federal Republic, Italy, and the Netherlands.
    An additional factor of possible importance in timber consumption is the
existence of national forestry operations. This might explain the relatively
high consumption in Canada, Finland, Sweden, and the U.S.S.R. These
countries have highly developed timber and furniture industries. Exports of
wood and timber products would have to be allowed for in order to find the
true level of domestic consumption.

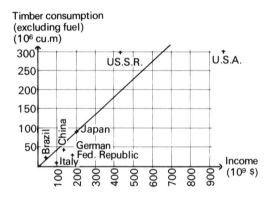

Figure 6.20. Timber consumption and income

6.9 The limits

Chapter 3 gave the norm that the annual consumption of resources should be
limited to one percent of reserves. For all sectors combined the potential
consumption can be determined from the relationships with income (see 6.8).
This aggregate consumption is then compared with the one percent norm to
indicate what economies are needed.
    The consumption of scarce materials allowable for housing is determined
according to the proportion of income normally spent on housing. But this
limitation does not relate to sand, gravel, cement, or clay. These are typical
building materials and are in such ample supply that there is no need to
restrict their use.
    No clear correlation was found between the percentage of income devoted
to housing and income level, per capita income, population growth, or the

percentage of the population moving into newly-built accommodation. The percentage is, however, lower on average in the poor countries than in the rich ones (2.7 percent and 4.8 percent respectively). Based on available figures, therefore, the relationship is as depicted in Figure 6.21.

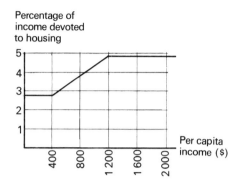

Figure 6.21. Percentages of income devoted to housing

As applied to the year 2020, it is found that in both poor and rich countries 4.8 percent of income is devoted to housing. With a building requirement of 44.8 and 11.4 million homes respectively, the average price of building is $ 12,418 in the poor countries and $ 22,995 in the rich ones. On the further assumption that building workers' wages will develop in parallel with the average income, we find average hourly rates in the year 2020 of $ 3.99 in the poor countries and $ 5.03 in the rich ones.

The rise in basic material prices must also be taken into account. The total increase deriving from the general depletion of natural resources (see Figure 6.5) is deducted from income via an increase in the capital coefficient. An indication of the rise in prices of individual materials is given by the relative rise in the cost of one particular material compared with the overall rise. The prices of copper, zinc, and aluminium are rising especially steeply. As available quantities are small, this does not have much effect on building costs.

The model in any case uses constant prices (1970 dollars), eliminating the effects of inflation. In interpreting the results, therefore, price increases since then should be taken into account. Retail price index figures and building cost per housing unit are published monthly by the Netherlands Central Bureau of Statistics (CBS). This is the source of the information in Table 6.1.

Table 6.1. Retail price and building cost indices 1970-76

	Retail prices	Building costs per housing unit
1970	100	100
1971	108	114
1972	116	123
1973	125	138
1974	137	156
1975	151	168
1976	165	183

6.10 Simulation model results

Table 6.2 summarises the results from the model. Most of them have already been discussed in the text. The following is added regarding consumption of materials.

The quantities in the table indicate how much is available per house. This depends on the following factors: aggregate consumption of materials, possible economies, the proportion reserved for housing, and the number of houses required. In 1970 over twenty times as much was available for a rich house as for a poor one; in the year 2020 there will be only twice as much. Income redistribution therefore makes a relatively much larger amount available for a poor house. But the depletion of reserves means that the poor lose in absolute terms except in the case of steel and energy.

Table 6.2. Simulation model results

Item	Unit	Poor				Rich			
		1970	1980	2000	2020	1970	1980	2000	2020
1 Population	pers.	2.5×10^9	3.1×10^9	4.6×10^9	5.4×10^9	1.2×10^9	1.5×10^9	1.7×10^9	1.7×10^9
2 Per capita income	$	169	331	1,182	2,166	2,360	3,000	3,260	3,157
3 Percentage rich income transferred	%					0.5	2.0	3.1	1.5
4 Income transfers	$					16×10^9	83×10^9	176×10^9	86×10^9
5 Income distribution factor	1	1	1	1	1	13.97	9.1	2.8	1.5
6 Percentage of income spent on housing	%	2.8	2.8	4.8	4.8	4.8	4.8	4.8	4.8
7 Maximum cost per house	$	1,248	1,200	6,370	12,418	25,439	20,350	19,691	22,995
8 Average density of occupation	pers.	5.3	5.2	4.6	3.7	4.5	4.4	3.9	3.6
9 Number of houses to be built (incl. renovations)	1	9.4×10^6	24.8×10^6	43.4×10^6	44.8×10^6	5.3×10^6	9.8×10^6	13.7×10^6	11.4×10^6
10 Building workers' hourly rates	$	0.45	0.87	2.71	3.99	4.76	5.88	5.77	5.03
11 Steel	kg	161	149	278	276	3,275	2,830	1,081	581
12 Aluminium	kg	4	1	3	3	92	34	11	5
13 Copper	kg	3.3	0.5	0.9	0.8	67	9	2	1
14 Lead	kg	1.3	0.2	0.3	0.2	27	2.7	0.8	0.5
15 Zinc	kg	2.1	0.2	0.3	0.3	42.4	2.8	0.8	0.5
16 Energy	kg CE	2,610	2,420	12,560	26,180	53,270	46,040	40,560	47,200

7. Designing within the limits

7.1 Building estimate

The simulation model results indicate a number of important limits which will apply to houses to be built in the period 1970 to 2020. The architect will be bound by three restrictions:

1. a maximum amount which includes cost of materials and man-hours and other building costs;
2. a maximum quantity of scarce resources in the case of steel, aluminium copper, lead, and zinc;
3. a maximum amount of energy, which includes on-site consumption and the energy required for manufacturing the building materials.

Energy is not used only to build the house, however; even in temperate zones the energy used for heating will be many times that needed for building. In order to limit this, a fourth restriction should be added:

4. the design and detailed specification of the house will have to ensure that a maximum annual loss of heat is not exceeded.

Designs of buildings are often based on a *specification of requirements*. It establishes the design criteria and the future occupant's needs and wishes. By analogy, the list of restrictions applicable to housing construction in the year 2020 has been called the *specification of limits*. Within these limits, the architect will have to design houses, using his own concepts, skills, and experience and taking account of current views.

To prevent this list of uncommon limitations becoming unwieldy, a method was developed with which a satisfactory design can be made effectively and efficiently.

The present chapter works out in succession the points of departure for the building estimates, the limitations on energy consumption for space heating, the specification of limits, and the design method. Lastly, there are a number of designs for houses in order to test the value of the system in practice.

The model gives the amounts of money, scarce materials, and energy available per house in the year 2020. The budget does not cover the cost of land or preparing the site where this relates to the infra-structure or public services such as roads, drains or piping, and cables.

The available amounts on which the calculations are based can be divided into a net budget (the total cost of wages and materials) and a variety of additional cost items. These include recurrent items (such as depreciation of equipment, management and supervision, loss of interest, and insurance), technical installations, and taxation. Careful analysis shows that the influence these items have on the total cost per house is fairly constant. To make the calculations as simple as possible and to enable the projects to be compared, the specification of limits will use net budgets; all additional general cost items will be deducted as fixed percentages from the available amounts. It will also be ascertained how much material and energy the additional work uses. This will ultimately have to be allowed for in the specification of limits. The influence of each of the above factors will be illustrated by reference to the customary procedure for preparing building cost estimates.

The net budget is taken as x. This comprises wages (including social security costs and wage tax) and materials used at the site. First of all, some customary costs of carrying out the work have to be deducted from the total budget.

Table 7.1. Costs, materials, and energy in recurrent items and general expenses

Item	Cost as percentage of net budget	Materials	Energy (kg CE)
Cost of connecting technical installations	1		100
Small carpentry jobs, setting out, measuring, repairs, cleaning, regular maintenance, etc.	5	Wood, plastic (provisional)	
Management, supervision, insurance, depreciation of equipment, loss of interest, and general expenses	15		
Contractor's remuneration	5		
Total	26		100

These are grouped together as *recurrent items*, as specified in Table 7.1. The usual procedure would be to add a fixed percentage of profit for the contractor to the sum-total of net cost and recurrent items; in practice this is usually 10 percent. In view of the levelling up postulated by us, however, (see 3.6.2) this would lead to discrepancies between incomes. So this percentage is replaced by 5 percent contractor's remuneration under recurrent items. Costs are expressed in the table as percentages of net budget (x).

Technical installations for heating, gas, electricity, and water have so far been disregarded. They are usually supplied by third parties and shown separately in the estimates. As with recurrent costs, the cost of such installations can be fairly simply expressed as a percentage. In order to simplify the estimates, plumbing and drainage are included as technical installations.

Regarding the use of materials, we are faced with a number of problems arising from the limits which the model imposes for the year 2020. The shortage of natural resources made it necessary to apply the following principles:

1. As the aggregate amount of steel available is extremely small, mainly plastic substitutes are assumed to be used for installations. For central heating equipment 100 kg steel is provided.
2. The amount of copper available is insufficient to make a conventional electrical installation in which this material is an indispensable conductor. We shall assume that usable alternatives will be available in the future (3.3.1.3).
3. Hot and cold water installations are based on plastic piping. This is already used in practice on a modest scale.
4. The available amounts of lead and zinc are so slight that they can hardly be considered for use in the building industry.

Table 7.2 gives the cost of installations and also the consumption of materials and energy by which the amount available for houses in rich and poor countries has to be reduced.

The total cost of construction, recurrent items, and technical installations is $x + 0.26x + 0.18x = 1.44x$. This aggregate amount is the basis for calculating the architect's fee. As the levelling up of incomes would be frustrated if prevailing charges were maintained, this fee is likewise replaced by a remuneration, which also covers designing and drawing etc., of 8 percent of the aggregate amount.

Table 7.2. Costs, materials, and energy for technical installations

Item	Cost as per-centage of net budget	Materials	Energy (kg CE)
Heating, refrigeration	6	100 kg steel	100
		plastic	500
Electrical installation	3	0.8/1 kg copper	100
Gas	1	plastic	50
Hot and cold water	2	plastic	150
Plumbing	4	ceramics	50
		plastic	
Drainage	2	ceramics	50
		plastic	
		provisional:	
		0.24/0.5 kg lead	
		0.31/0.53 kg zinc	
Total	18		1000

In addition, special provisions are often needed against adverse local conditions. Extremes of climate, poor soil structure, or the possibility of earthquakes may vary the cost per house. An adjustment of 3 percent of the aggregate cost is reserved for this and 900 kg CE is deducted from the available energy.

Lastly, tax is charged on all the costs. As nearly all countries have a tax with the same financial effect as a Value Added or Sales Tax, the percentage – 12 percent – in the Netherlands in the reference year 1970 has been applied.

Table 7.3 is a recapitulation of the general costs and their significance with respect to the budget. The aggregate cost (sum-total of net cost estimates, recurrent items and technical installations) is y. The total cost per house is therefore 179 percent of the net budget. Hence, the net price as a basis for the specification of limits will have to be 100: 179, or 55.86 percent of the total budget.

As regards materials, steel must be cut by 100 kg, while copper, lead, and zinc are banned.

The energy available per house must be reduced by a total of $100 + 1,000 + 900 = 2,000$ kg CE.

Table 7.3. Building cost estimates as a percentage of net budget

Item	Cost as percentage of net budget
NET BUDGET (x)	100
Recurrent items	26
Technical installations	18
	———— +
AGGREGATE COST (y)	144
Architect's remuneration: 8% of y	11.52
Adjustment: 3% of y	4.32
	———— +
Total	159.84
Tax: 12% of 159.84	19.18
	———— +
TOTAL COST	179.02

7.2 Energy consumption and heat insulation

As stated at the beginning of this chapter, houses will have to be designed so that a permitted annual loss of heat owing to space heating is not exceeded. The limit for this is calculated as follows.

Van Bremen (1974) says that 20 percent of Western Europe's energy is consumed by domestic users and that 75 percent of this is for space heating and ventilation, i.e. 15 percent of the total. The total amount of energy available per inhabitant per annum is found from the ratio between income and energy consumption (see 6.8.1). The amount available for the rich in the year 2020 is 6,661 kg CE *per person* and for the poor nations 4,570 kg CE. Assuming the 15 percent mentioned above remains unchanged, 3,600 and 2,536 kg CE respectively will be available *per house* for space heating and ventilation in the year 2020. Expressed as heat units, the figures for the specification of limits are then 25.2×10^6 kcal for a house in a rich country and 17.8×10^6 kcal for one in a poor country.

The loss in efficiency of energy consumption is about 40 percent; the remaining 60 percent goes in heat transmission. Other influences, such as losses through ventilation and gains from sunshine, lighting, domestic equipment, and heat emitted by the human body, practically cancel one another out and can be disregarded for calculations of a general nature.

In practice the loss in transmission is calculated with k, the heat loss in kcal per sq.m per hour per degree C. For instance, k for an uninsulated cavity wall is 1.7. For single and double glazing it is 5 and 2.7 respectively. Appendix D gives the values of k for a number of conventional building structures. In order to have a broad check on the thermal properties of a house at an early stage in the design process, an average value of k is applied. Let us now calculate the maximum permitted values of k for two types of houses in rich countries. The basic data are:

- 40% loss in efficiency;
- an average of 5,100 hours heating a year;
- an average difference of 14° C between indoor and outdoor temperatures.

A detached house with a floor surface of 100 sq.m and a total outer surface of 300 sq.m may then have a maximum average value of k of:

$$\frac{25.2 \times 10^6 \times 0.60}{300 \times 5,100 \times 14} = 0.7$$

For a terraced house with a total outer surface of 210 sq.m, it will be:

$$\frac{25.2 \times 10^6 \times 0.60}{210 \times 5,100 \times 14} = 1.$$

7.3 The specification of limits

Table 7.4 gives the limits applying in the year 2020 to building houses on the basis of an economic life of 50 years.

The maximum permitted cost of building houses in rich countries with an average of 3.6 occupants is $ 22,995. The results of the model are stated in standard 1970 dollars.

According to the model an income ratio of 1.5:1 will be reached between rich and poor nations by the year 2020. But this does not imply absolute income equality in these nations themselves. This study assumes a maximum spread in incomes of 1:2 in both rich and poor nations (see 3.6.2). The net budget for an average house in rich countries can therefore fluctuate between $ 8,563 and $ 17,127.

In fixing the limits differences in family structures must be taken into account. Separate limits are therefore given for single persons and for families of 2, 3, or more persons.

Table 7.4. Limits for houses in the year 2020

Number of occupants	Net budget	Maximum			
		Materials (kg)		Energy for	Space heating (10^6 kcal per annum)
		Steel	Aluminium	Building (kg CE)	
Rich:					
1	4,167- 8,333	150-300	1.5-3	15,000-30,000	8.5-17
2	5,858-11,715	215-431	2.2-4.4	21,333-42,667	11.7-23.4
3	7,549-15,097	281-562	2.9-5.8	27,667-55,333	14.9-29.8
3.6	8,563-17,127	321-642	3.3-6.7	31,467-62,933	16.8-33.6
4	9,240-18,479	396-693	3.6-7.2	34,000-68,000	18.1-36.2
5	10,931-21,861	412-825	4.3-8.6	40,333-80,666	21.3-42.6
Poor:					
1	2,083- 4,167	60-120	1 -2	10,000-20,000	6 -12
2	3,024- 6,049	81-163	1.4-2.7	12,760-25,521	8.1-16.3
3	3,966- 7,931	103-205	1.7-3.5	15,221-31,907	10.3-20.6
3.7	4,624- 9,249	117-235	2 -4	17,453-34,907	11.9-23.7
4	4,907- 9,814	124-248	2.1-4.2	18,281-36,563	12.5-24.9
5	5,848-11,696	145-290	2.5-5	21,042-42,084	14.6-29.2

It would be unfair to allocate accommodation in direct proportion to the number of tenants. Whatever the size of the family, every house has a given minimum of certain utilities, including sanitation and cooking facilities. There is no need for a house for five persons to have five times the floor surface of a house for one. Proportionate allocation would allow an average of only $ 3,568 for a house for one person. This would mean that single persons' houses up to present standards would be out of the question. Hence the limits allow a net budget of up to $ 8,333 for a single person's house.

Regarding the use of scarce materials and energy, section 7.1 showed that the steel available per house must be reduced by 100 kg and the energy by 2,000 kg CE. As with the net budgets, the limits applicable to materials and energy are also differentiated according to numbers of occupants; the same applies to energy for space heating.

On the above basis, the limits which will have to be observed in the design can now be calculated. They are listed in Table 7.4. The estimates must allow for an hourly wage of $ 5.00 in the rich nations and $ 4.00 in the poor ones. Lastly, the cost of materials is based on 1970 market prices in the Netherlands.

7.4 Design methods

The design method is based on existing cost-conscious design techniques. Their object is to give the architect an overall check on the costing implications of every design decision. Tables are used containing data for 'element estimates', i.e. costs of complete constructional elements or parts of buildings.

Our method integrates the cost of materials and man-hours and the use of energy and resources. All costs of materials are based on constant 1970 prices (see 6.9). In order to compare all designs on the same basis, the following tables are used:

1. Estimates of costs of constructional elements, Bouwcentrum, Rotterdam (1970).
2. Tables from *Begrotingen voor de bouwwereld* (Building cost estimates), Jelsma (1973). These give the man-hours required for every building operation.
3. Standard building material prices from Misset's *Bouwwereld* (1970).
4. Data on energy in building materials (see 3.6) expressed as kg CE per ton product.

5. Table of insulating values of the most common types of construction (see Appendix D).

The design process is divided into stages so that the necessary checks can be made at each stage. The method is illustrated in Figure 7.1.

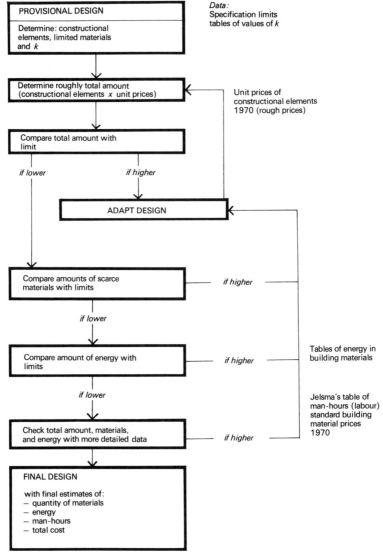

Figure 7.1. Design method

7.5 Designs for testing the specification of limits and the design method

A number of houses were designed to test the limits and the design method outlined in this chapter. 25 students of architecture at the National Higher Institute of Architecture and Town Planning (Nationaal Hoger Instituut voor Bouwkunst en Stedebouw), Antwerp, spent a specially organised working-week on this. One reason for this was to find out whether the system could be used by architects completely unfamiliar with it.

The instructions were: design a house or a number of housing units located in North-West Europe for construction in the year 2020. There was a choice of four types:
– a detached house,
– a terraced house,
– a rural cluster (about 12 units with not more than two storeys),
– an urban cluster.
The main problem during the week was to break away from existing design routines and patterns of thought. This led in most cases to the use of standardised elements and mechanisation, with the consequence that energy and steel consumption was exceptionally high at first and the limits were greatly exceeded.

Nevertheless, the system itself worked satisfactorily and produced reasonable results within a short time. Four designs were selected for publication. Because of the limited time available, the heat insulation requirements were disregarded.

7.5.1 Detached house (Design: C. Bresseleers and B. Menten)

This is a design for an average house for rich countries. Its principle is brick piers with composite wooden walls and outside wall elements; reinforced concrete footings and ground floor; wooden roof; net floor surface 97 sq.m. including storage; suitable for four persons (Figure 7.2).

Condensed estimates

Wages 1,492 × $ 5	$ 7,460
Materials	$ 4,414
NET COST	$ 11,874
Steel	496 kg
Energy	10,000 kg CE

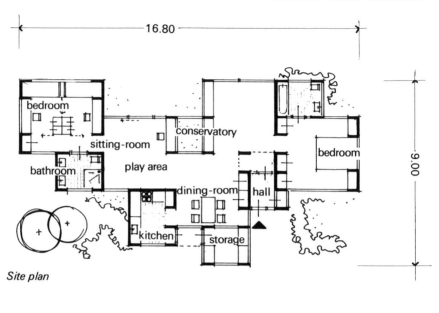

Site plan

front elevation

Figure 7.2 Detached house

7.5.2 Terraced house (Design: J. Ertzingen and G. Pijl)

This design features a highly standardised main structure. The site plan can be varied by using interchangeable built-in elements. The load-bearing separating walls are of brick, the lower-storey floor is reinforced concrete, while the upper-storey floor and roof are of wood. The total floor area for four persons is 95 sq.m excluding storage (Figure 7.3).

Condensed estimates

Wages 1,297 × $ 5	$ 6,485
Materials	$ 3,675
NET COST	$ 10,160
Steel	450 kg
Energy	8,350 kg CE

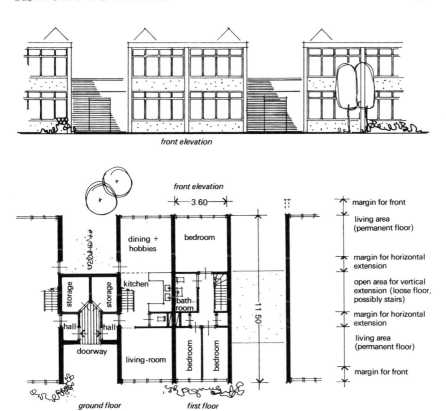

Figure 7.3. Urban terraced house

7.5.3 Rural cluster (Design: E. Binneman and P. Peeters)

The cluster consists of 13 houses grouped around a common open space. They are all designed on the same lines but vary in size. The principal materials are brick for loadbearing parts and wood for floors and separating walls. A house for four persons has 126 sq.m of floor (Figure 7.4).

Condensed estimates (four persons)

Wages 1,653 × $ 5	$ 8,265
Materials	$ 4,532
NET COST	$ 12,797
Steel	410 kg
Energy	9,780 kg CE

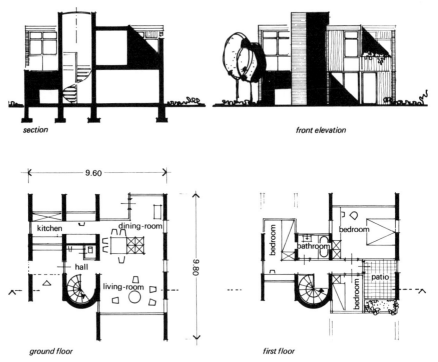

Figure 7.4. Rural clusters

7.5.4 Urban cluster (Design: M. Buytaert, D. de Vocht, and P. Meester)

This block is intended for families of different sizes and single persons (about 35 persons in all). There are common locations for washing machines and for recreation. Outside locations are within the cluster, so that various clusters can be built close together. Heights vary from one to three storeys. Materials are reinforced concrete, bricks, and wood. A house for four persons has 115 sq.m of floor.

Condensed estimates (four persons)

Wages 1,335 × $ 5	$ 6,675
Materials	$ 4,231
NET COST	$ 10,906
Steel	410 kg
Energy	20,000 kg CE

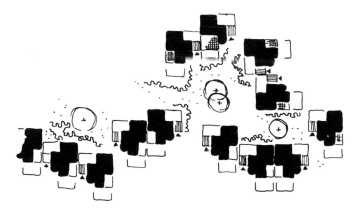

Figure 7.5. Group of clusters

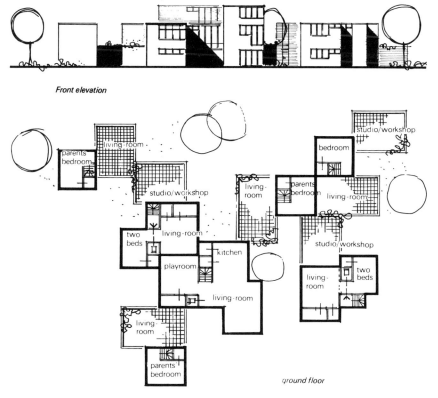

Figure 7.6. Urban cluster

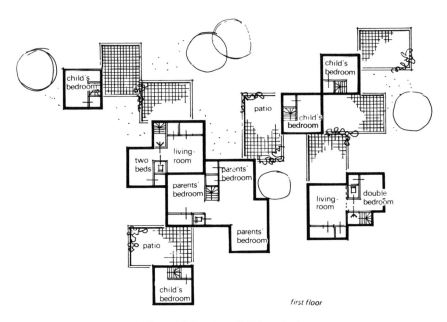

Figure 7.6. (continued) Urban cluster

8. The projects

8.1 Urban terraced house (Design: Frits Mastenbroek)

A detached house, the ideal of many, is financially beyond the reach of most people especially in conurbations where land is very expensive. An alternative is a terraced house, which is much cheaper to build; footings, separating walls, and roofs can be built for a number of houses at once and usually less land is required.

Originally, small-scale materials were used: bricks, wood, and so on. It was possible, though not always easy, to divide the house up differently. The small-scale materials also allowed a great variety of outside walls, and individual houses or small groups of houses were clearly distinguishable.

Another aspect of the terraced house is the social contact with other residents in the block. This is very evident even now in small communities like those still found in most villages. People of all ages with different family structures live in them. Differences in social or financial status do not count. The doctor knows the baker, the carpenter the gardener, the factory-hand the notary, and vice versa. There are so many meeting-points that there is little anonymity. People identify themselves with the community. There is a close involvement with nature because many people have gardens; this contrasts with high-rise flats, where there is usually no direct contact with greenery.

For many people, therefore, the terraced house comes near to their ideal, and such homes are likely to become very important by the year 2020.

But there are also considerable drawbacks to terraced houses. The wish to build cheaply has greatly encouraged the process of industrialisation with a consequent uniformity. The prefabrication of unvaried series of elements gives a very impersonal effect. Entire districts are sometimes built with only two or three different types of houses all with the same layout. There is hardly any scope for modification. All this makes the occupants' social structure disagreeably uniform. Outwardly, the houses have bare, flat fronts. The use of large-scale concrete elements make the houses very inflexible inside. An upper-storey floor, for instance, consists of three elements already comprising all the facilities (staircase opening, electricity cables, water and waste pipes).

In drawing up specifications for urban terraced houses in the year 2020, past errors should be avoided wherever possible. The limits indicated by the simulation model for the cost of houses and the use of scarce materials also have to be observed.

The design must, moreover, stress the favourable aspects of terraced houses. The possibility of participation by the future occupants should be allowed for. The structure should permit occupants to decide the type of home they want, within certain limits, and those in charge should be favourably disposed towards this. The architect will have to act as a mentor to individual occupants. By consulting together, the most ideal type of home can be decided upon for everyone, within the scope of the terrace and, in a broader sense, that of the district.

Inside, it will have to be possible to obtain the desired layout by simple means. Outside, it must be possible to adapt the house to changing conditions. For instance, the dimensions of the footings could allow for extensions within specific limits. The design should also allow the house to be made bigger or smaller by combining it with another house or by splitting it. A couple starting a family, or parents whose children have grown up and moved out will not always have to seek accommodation elsewhere but can arrange for a suitable alternative in the same street or district. This will cater for the strong local ties which particularly affect old people. It is very important for such people to be able to stay in a familiar neighbourhood and not to be forced into homes for the aged.

8.1.1 Specification of requirements

To avoid the drawbacks of present terraced houses, those in the year 2020 should comply with the following standards:
– their acoustics should be close to those of the ideal, the detached house;
– their design and heat insulation should cut the energy consumption of present houses by a half;
– inside and outside, they should be flexible within given limits. The site plan should be able to meet a variety of needs;
– their layout should allow them to be split up or combined by simple means;
– privacy should receive special attention.

8.1.2 Principal measures

Sound insulation

Good sound insulation is provided by the following means:
- load-bearing cavity walls which, including the inner leaves, are built on thick felt on the footings.
- at the centre of the load-bearing wall the outside masonry has a narrow gap from top to bottom, filled with a compound for instance.
- one side of the double loadbearing wall is wiped down with mortar on the inside to prevent sound leaking through any gaps in the brickwork.
- there is a gap with foam rubber pressed in, formed with a rabbet, between the roofing sheets at the centre of the load-bearing wall (only the roof covering is continuous).
- where the roofing sheets are laid on the load-bearing wall, special precautions are taken to stop sound leakage.

The design provides for comfort with respect to sound insulation indoors. For instance, the wooden staircase is kept away from the living area, and the lavatory and shower are separated from the bedrooms (see Figures 8.3, 8.4, and 8.5). A half-brick wall or a brick cupboard-wall can be built as a sound barrier between the bedrooms. The upstairs floor is 19 cm-thick concrete. Combined with carpeting, this ensures the very good sound insulation essential if the houses are split.

Heat insulation

Good heat insulation is provided by the following means:
- compared with Dutch standards, the houses have little glazing (see Figure 8.2);
- the lower-storey floor has a fireproof layer of insulating plastic (3 cm thick) on its underside;
- the cavity walls are filled with plastic insulating blankets (10 cm thick);
- windows and other light openings have insulating glazing,
- the roof has a fireproof plastic insulating layer (3 cm thick).

Flexibility

The design provides for flexibility inside and outside as a built-in standard.

For instance, extra foundation beams are already provided during construction as shown with dotted lines in Figure 8.1. These can be used to extend the house if required. (The architect can then play an important part in advising on style, as mentioned above.) Unit No. 2 (see Figure 8.3), for instance, has an extra room over the storage space.

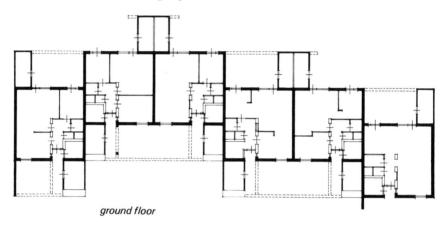

ground floor

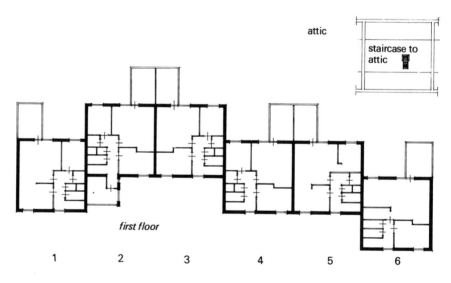

first floor

Figure 8.1. Block of urban terraced houses

Flexibility inside the house is provided for as follows:
– the possibility of demolishing separating walls as shown by broken lines in

the plan giving the measurements (Figure 8.6);
- the fitting of kitchen supply and waste pipes on the ground floor at both back and front (Figure 8.4);
- the fitting of supply and waste pipes for a kitchen at the rear when pouring the first floor (Figure 8.3).

Combining and splitting up

To allow people to move in their own streets or within their own districts, the houses are designed so that they can be split up or combined vertically by simple means. Splitting or combining horizontally has been avoided because the loadbearing cavity wall would have to be broken out, which would affect sound insulation.

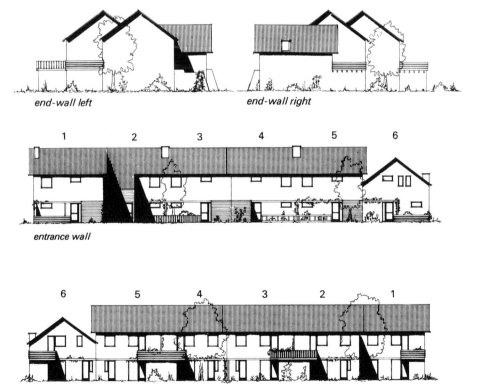

end-wall left   *end-wall right*

entrance wall

garden-side wall

Figure 8.2 Urban terraced houses (outside walls)

The single-family units can easily be split up or combined by modifying the entrance section. If the entrance to an upper unit is replaced by a wooden partition and the half-brick wall demolished, an entrance to a four-roomed unit is made. The design provides for this, and the house may seem rather extravagant at first. It suddenly has two lots of storage accommodation and two showers. But if the ground-floor shower is used as a wash-room and the store at the rear for hobbies, the house will have a high use value (Figure 8.4). Even the patio designed specially for the upper unit is a welcome addition.

ground floor

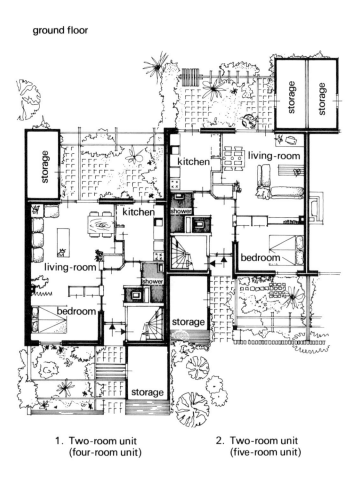

1. Two-room unit
(four-room unit)

2. Two-room unit
(five-room unit)

Figure 8.3. Urban terraced house (1 and 2)

Units 1 to 5 (see Figures 8.4 and 8.5) show various possibilities. Unit 6 allows for the possibility of using the ground floor as a neighbourhood facility, while the upstairs can be fitted out as a bachelor flat (see Figure 8.5).

Privacy

Partly because of the high window and the front garden, it is practically impossible for people to look in from the street (see Figure 8.2). The storage accommodation at the back and front and the separations between the patios also heighten the sense of privacy. The use value of the houses is further increased by the long gardens at the back, where there is room enough to plant tall trees for shelter.

first floor

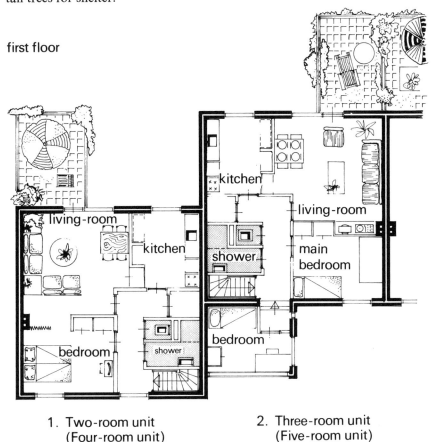

1. Two-room unit
   (Four-room unit)

2. Three-room unit
   (Five-room unit)

Figure 8.3. (Continued)

8.1.3 Constructional details

Dimensions:

- dimensions are modular, horizontally and vertically.

Structure:

- footings: sand-lime bricks on firmed bed of sand;
- sand-lime brickwork inside and out, chosen because of low energy consumption;
- lower-storey floor: joists and sheets;
- second-storey floor: 19 cm prefabricated prestressed concrete slabs;

ground floor

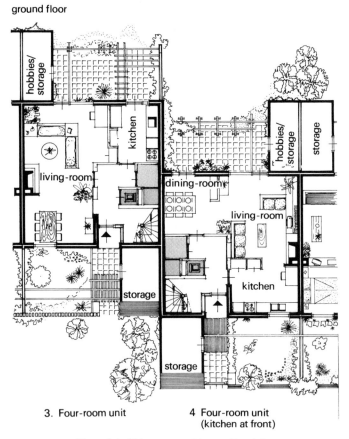

3. Four-room unit   4 Four-room unit (kitchen at front)

Figure 8.4. Urban terraced house (3 and 4)

3 Four-room unit   4 Four-room unit

Figure 8.4. (Continued)

– attic floor: wooden joists and sheets;
– roof: purlin roof with insulating roofing sheets;
– bituminous roof covering;
– door and window frames: North European deal.

Heating:

– individual hot-air installation in attic; the air is blown upwards and downwards through ducts in the pipe and cable shaft and channels in the concrete floor; the advantage is that the air can be partly changed even with
  the windows closed.

Electricity:

– switches and wall sockets incorporated in special skirting;
– lighting is fitted in rails along the walls; no ceiling lights.

General:

– PVC meter cupboards outside the house near the front garden entrance (see
  Figure 8.3).

8.1.4 Estimates

Finally, the estimates are given for a four-room unit, with 142.5 sq.m of floor (30 sq.m of this for attic and storage). See Table 8.1.

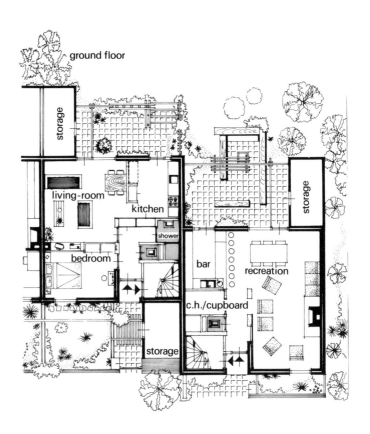

5 Two-room unit
   (Four-room unit)

6 Recreation area
   (Four-room unit)

First floor

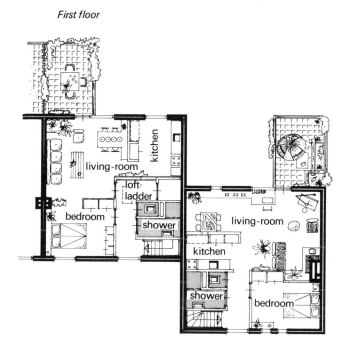

5 Two-room unit
   (Four-room unit)

6 Two-room unit
   (Four-room unit)

Figure 8.5. Urban terraced house (5 and 6)

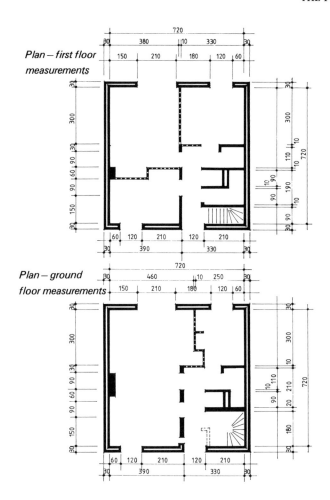

Figure 8.6. Urban terraced house (measurements)

Table 8.1 Estimates for a four-roomed house

Item	Quantity		Labour hours	wages	Materials ($)	Energy (kg CE)
Site work Earth moved by machine	202	cu.m	5.5	27.67	87.50	
Footings Sand-lime brick; mortar	12	cu.m	78	392.38	166.54	1,850
Masonry Outside load-bearing and inside walls; separating brickwork including mortar (16 hrs per 1000 bricks)	33,750		540	2,716.50	761.94	
Pointing Outside walls and part of inside (hall, stair walls, storage space); incl. mortar	320	cu.m	64	321.96	12.00	50
Concreting Upper-storey floor, small concrete jobs, paving and drainage tiles	11.3	cu.m	32	160.98	609.72	595
Carpentry Ground floor, first floor, roof; outside and inside door and window frames; roof of storage space; stairs etc.	9.3	cu.m	177	890.41	1,778.91	4
Wall plastering Only in living-room, bedrooms, kitchen, shower, and W.C., including mortar	140	sq.m	63	316.93	44.03	452
Tiling Flooring and wall tiles, cornices and window ledges, including mortar	68	sq.m	69	347.11	142.64	133
Glazing and painting Except store doors, double glazing throughout; impregnate woodwork plus two coats of stain;	4 + 16 sq.m		4	20.12	191.11	} 440
spray ceilings with texture paint	70	kg	29	145.89	75.00	
Roof covering Shingles on roof; single layer of roof covering	70	sq.m	56	281.71	165.28	} 1,350
over storage spaces (6 kg/sq.m)	16	sq.m	8	40.25	26.67	
Plastics Gutter 16 m run	3.2 kg		4	20.12	16.67	
Glass wool blankets 10 cm thick in cavities 20 kg/cu.m (450 kg)	225	sq.m	17	85.52	82.64	810
Insulation under first-storey floor Insulation on roofing sheets 3 cm	3.6 cu.m					72
Total			1,145.5	5,767.53	4,160.65	5,756

Total cost of materials and wages: $ 9,928

Conclusions

An urban terraced house can be built to comply with the specification and limits. Living in such a house can be just as pleasant as in a detached house. Sound and heat insulation of the terraced house as designed are of a high standard. Inside and outside there is ample provision for flexibility. The use of small-scale elements and small series makes plenty of variety possible in the neighbourhood. Taking into account its comparatively low price, the urban terraced house presents attractive prospects for the future.

8.2 A house in a poor country (Design: Piet Bennehey)

Kloos (1972) came to the conclusion that in order to achieve harmony between a community's social structure and the material form of the home:
– less specialised and more all-purpose houses were required;
– these should be adaptable to changing conditions and circumstances;
– the occupant should regain the freedom to design and perhaps build his house the way he wishes.

If we agree with the last point, it is hardly possible to design a house for someone else, especially a house in the future in an unfamiliar society. The main purpose of this project, therefore, is to illustrate the technical and financial possibilities in the year 2020 on the basis of the simulation-model results.

Key:
1 Desert (Sahara)
2 Desert steppes (Sahel)
3 Grassland steppes
4 Light tropical forest and savanna
5 Tropical rain forest

Figure 8.7. Location of house in Africa

8.2.1 Location

The second test case led to the choice of a house in West Africa in a rural area in climatic region 4 (see Figure 8.7).

In these areas large families often live together (grandparents, parents, children, and grandchildren). They live in huts grouped round a central space; the head of the family has the biggest hut. This mode of living has evolved in the course of time.

The inner area is used for communal activities such as pounding grain, keeping chickens, cooking, getting together, and playing. As a whole it has a defensive character: it can be closed off from the outside (see Figure 8.8). The principal reason is an Islam tradition forbidding women to appear in public.

The design and construction used in the test case have a number of drawbacks, mainly of a technical nature:
- the life of the house is fairly limited;
- the roof will last for only two to five years and is flammable;
- the walls will crack because there are no footings;
- access to light and air is inadequate because there are no windows;
- in our eyes the earthen floor is not particularly hygienic;
- there are no lavatory or washing facilities.

8.2.2 Specification of limits

Let us examine what improvements are possible by the year 2020 based on the results of the model. It is assumed that the family community will still be about the same as it is now. A rather arbitrary choice has been made of a community consisting of grandparents, man and wife with three children, man and wife with one child, and a childless couple. The design has to meet the following requirements:
- the existing community grouping is to be maintained;
- the principle of living in an enclosure is adopted;
- the design must be based as far as possible on the situation of the *poorest poor* in the year 2020;
- the climate must be taken into account.

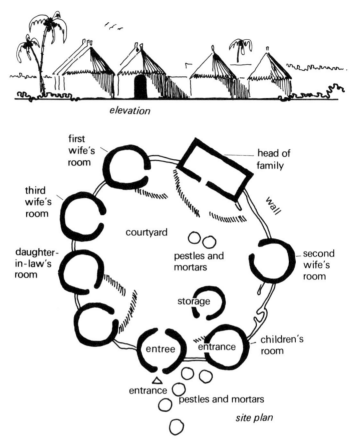

Figure 8.8 Traditional group of huts in rural West Africa

With the limits for the year 2020 found in Chapter 7 the net budget can be calculated as follows:

	poorer poor	richer poor
Grandparents	$ 3,024	$ 6,049
Man and wife with three children	5,848	11,696
Man and wife with one child	3,966	7,931
Man and wife	3,024	6,049
Total	$ 15,862	$ 31,725

The energy and materials available for twelve persons are:

Energy	$12/3.7 \times 26{,}180$		=	84,908	kg CE
Aluminum	$12/3.7 \times$	3	=	9.7	kg
Steel	$12/3.7 \times$	276	=	895	kg
Copper	$12/3.7 \times$	0.8	=	2.6	kg
Lead	$12/3.7 \times$	0.24	=	0.8	kg
Zinc	$12/3.7 \times$	0.31	=	1	kg

The quantity of steel is based on the gross quantity available because the 100 kg reserve for heating is unnecessary in this case.

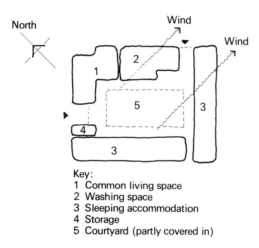

Key:
1 Common living space
2 Washing space
3 Sleeping accommodation
4 Storage
5 Courtyard (partly covered in)

Figure 8.9 Grouping of accommodation round courtyard

8.2.3 Design

Figure 8.9 shows how the accommodation is grouped around the central courtyard.

Siting at an angle of 45° to the prevailing Westerly winds provides good opportunities for ventilation, which are made better still by the location of the entrance. The odour-producing areas are to the North-East.

Louvres allow all rooms to be ventilated. Day-time activities take place mainly under the verandahs, round the courtyard, and in the somewhat cooler rooms to the North. The bedrooms are on the hot side but cool off fairly quickly after sunset.

The design is shown in Figure 8.10.

An attempt was made to let the occupants join in the building work wherever possible. On the whole, the design has been kept simple. All the work can be done by hand and no cranes are needed. The footings consist of a concrete strip (45 cm wide and 20 cm deep). Concrete blocks are cemented on this up to the underside of the floor. The floors are also made of reinforced concrete with a lightweight contraction netting ($\#$, $\varnothing$ 15-20). The load-bearing outside walls are built of 15 cm-thick gravel-concrete blocks, while the non-

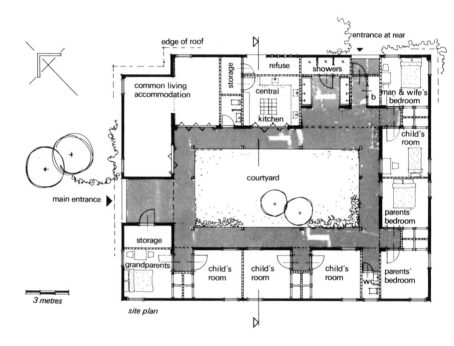

Figure 8.10. Plan for a house in West Africa

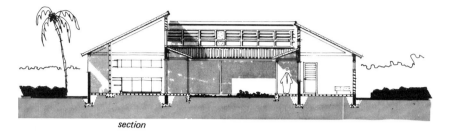

section

oblique projection

Figure 8.10. (continued)

loadbearing separating walls consist of 10 cm lightweight concrete blocks. Most walls are plastered. The outside walls have a cladding of wooden plates secured with steel ties. Windows, doors, and frames are made of wood, with glass or louvres.

Key:
1 Courtyard
2 Communal areas
3 Kitchen
4 Refuse
5 Washing
6 Showers
7 Storage
8 Bedroom

Figure 8.11. House in West Africa (divided)

The roof covering consists of glass-fibre reinforced cement sections made by sawing lengthways through pipes 45 cm in diameter and 4 to 5 metres long. This gives four sections spanning the entire gap and resting only on the load-bearing outside walls. This also allows changes to be made because the partition walls can be easily removed. The shed roof round the courtyard consists of light, corrugated cement sheeting, also glass-fibre reinforced.

It is also possible to split the entire structure into two parts later; an example is given in Figure 8.11.

8.2.4 Estimates

The estimates are given in Table 8.2. The total cost of wages and materials is $ 20,000.

Table 8.2 Estimates for a house in West Africa

Item	Quantity	Labour		Materials ($)	Energy (kg CE)
		hours	wages		
Site work		190	757.36	55.56	
Concreting	50 cu.m	340	1355.28	1015.00	3042
Masonry (concrete blocks)	70 cu.m	650	2590.97	1182.22	4171
Finishing walls/floors		352	1403.11	478.89	2695
Steel	874 kg	56	223.22	385.84	874
Reinforced cement roof covering tonnes	23 tonnes	363	1446.96	3128.61	5512
Wood	10 cu.m	258	1028.42	3441.67	4
Ceilings, insulation	131 sq.m	78	310.92	138.06	8420
Preservation			159.44	833.33	1206
Glazing	40 sq.m	40		68.61	298
Total		2327	9275.68	10727.79	26222

Conclusions

The major limiting factor is the net amount available. The amount available for the lowest income groups is still exceeded by $ 4167. Moreover, limitation of the use of steel was a restricting factor in design.

A conservative conclusion is that a reasonable house, based on the principles of the model, can be built in poor countries in the year 2020. Even if the figures are not entirely accurate, an idea of the possibilities is nevertheless given.

8.3 House with own supply facilities: Pyramid 2020 (Design: Willem van den Akker and Jan van Middelkoop)

Before presenting our own approach to a project, let us first examine some aspects of present-day Western society with a brief historical review of the progress of mankind in the past 6,000 to 10,000 years, culminating in our present civilisation. What influence has this had on future housing standards? These introductory observations should also be looked upon as a personal motivation. We fully realise that the conclusions are largely influenced by personal considerations.

8.3.1 Introduction

Primitive man

For a long time man lived in balance with his environment. Nature was both friend and foe. He was totally dependent on what nature had to offer but at the same time fought for survival against constant threats. He was unable to make any fundamental changes in these relationships but was part of a carefully balanced ecosystem.

Relationships between human beings were based on natural blood ties: children, relatives, and the tribe were the focal points. These relationships aimed at reproduction and survival, at continued functioning within the ecosystem. The principal occupation was seeking food. Man lived by hunting and collecting edible plants and fruit. To compete successfully with other more specialised hunters such as lions and tigers, he had to go hunting in groups. He was very cooperative from sheer necessity, and the common interest prevailing over that of the individual.

The various groups were completely autonomous and had no functional links. Each had its own customs and specific characteristics. It was hardly possible to change from group to group or place to place. Intruders in the group's hunting territory were a threat and were kept out. There were strong territorial bonds, and the close links with the soil were the only certainty for survival.

Development of farming and livestock raising

Because of man's readiness to cooperate and his adaptability, he was a very successful hunter. He spread almost all over the earth's surface. Where natural conditions were suitable he cultivated certain kinds of grain: wheat and barley in Mesopotamia, rice in Southern Asia, and maize in Central America. He also started domesticating animals such as goats, sheep, cattle, and pigs. The hunter and gatherer of food was becoming a farmer and raiser of livestock. In this way he was able to escape from a number of limitations which nature had imposed upon him. He was beginning to subdue and exploit nature.

He now not only had constant, regular supplies of food, but sometimes there were even surpluses. As a result, some members of the group began to devote all their time to matters not directly associated with food production; specialisation made its début. In a comparatively short time relationships between man and nature changed essentially. After this break, there were constant changes in social relationships; developments were taking place at an ever faster pace.

Urbanisation.

Overproduction and specialisation had sweeping consequences. They were the causes of increasing social complexity. Many new occupations arose that were no longer associated with the land. People simply looked for a favourable location to carry on business and exchanged their products for food and other commodities. A new concept came into being: trade, with the side-effects of profit and capital accumulation. This brought the need to protect property. Those who no longer had to produce food joined forces: the town was born.

Although the towns still retained close links with the arable land around them, they subordinated it to their needs. Bigger and bigger social units were formed. Towns grew in which it was no longer possible for everybody to know everybody else: the *impersonal society* had emerged.

As yet society was characterised by highly autonomous families with their own norms and ways of life; they were also self-governing. The family had close social control over its members. Extraneous influences were warded off and were of minor importance.

The increasing size of the towns led to greater subordination to the common interest. The social control of the family was largely lost. And lastly, the family also lost its elementary social and governing function. Some of the social functions were taken over by neighbourhood communities, within which people were able more or less to retain their own identities. The loss of the family's governing function also brought a need to introduce disciplinary laws and controls. This led to a need for new forms of government, which necessarily applied new, common norms. As the towns continued to grow, the gap between governors and the governed widened. The concentration of power and the consequent independent existence of the administration led to a high degree of absolutism.

For a long time urban society was characterised by a concentration of trade, crafts, and government. Following the industrial revolution, mechanisation, and mass-production, there was a strong concentration of employment, which was the beginning of still further urbanisation. Ultimately, the complexion of society was determined by conditions in the towns.

The world of modern Western man

Present-day society is overshadowed by the illusion that material progress is equivalent to happiness. The demand for prosperity is running ahead of industry's ability to provide it. But more and more people are realising that still more material prosperity will not automatically improve the quality of life. The industrial output this necessitates involves increasing specialisation. The consequent working conditions are monotonous, with a limited number of operations, a lack of involvement in the overall process, subjection to an imposed pace, and lack of scope for an individual (creative) contribution. The sacrifices we have to make for industrial production are factors which are not fully taken into account in economic thinking: clean surroundings, a richly varied environment, and healthy working conditions.

Urbanisation and industrialisation have alienated man from his natural habitat. He no longer lives on the land; this is doomed to produce food and supply materials for industry. In the cities, living, working, and recreation are physically and functionally segregated. Living is reduced to inhabiting a lo- cality equipped solely for this purpose, where there is no longer any place to work and too little space is set aside for recreation. This form of segregation, moreover, greatly encourages traffic and transport.

The concentration and up-scaling that follows increasing urbanisation has made for individual anonymity and lack of interest. These tendencies are inevitably leading to a situation in which man is becoming divorced from his environment, often resulting in complete isolation. Various forms of addic- tion, increasing aggressiveness, and crime are its symptoms. Degeneration and estrangement are reflected on a greater scale in exploitation, oppression, racial discrimination, genocide, and an uncontrolled arms race.

Conclusions

We can conclude that within this world pattern man is the victim of events whose disastrous consequences are loss of identity, worsening of interhuman relations, and alienation from the natural environment. If man wishes to continue functioning in lasting harmony with his fellow men and his environ- ment, this train of events will have to come to an end.

In order to restore the identity of the individual, the tendency towards up-scaling will have to be stopped. In a functionally separated, large-scale urbanised environment, the individual has no opportunity to become known, identified, or acknowledged. The largest unit within which every individual is reasonably acquainted with the other members consists of about 500 people. Within a community of 10,000 we believe it is still possible to be identifiable to some extent. Within such an urban unit enough social functions can be fulfilled to ensure a proper level of services (education, health care, and so on).

Down-scaling would create a climate in which it is quite possible to integrate such functions as living, working, food supply, care for the aged. And the family, the smallest social unit of all, can fully resume its educative, nurturing, and recreational functions.

8.3.2 Principles for the design

Relationship between man and nature:

Every family will have to have enough land available to supply part of their own food requirements. This will reinstate the relationship between man and nature.

Awareness of one's own situation within the environment may be a major factor in modifying attitudes to environmental problems. It is also a means of meeting present needs for recreation.

The amount of land this requires is by no means excessive. A lack of space is often emotional rather than real. We have seen population forecasts for the Netherlands for the year 2000 dropping from 20 million to 15 million or less in a short time. Stabilisation is near, and there may even be a decline. The agricultural situation has also changed. Much farmland has even become unprofitable, partly through overproduction.

Of the land area of the Netherlands (see Figure 8.12), 10.9 percent is used for housing, traffic, industry, and so on; 14.2 percent is woods and countryside, while 74.9 percent is under cultivation. Only about 2 percent is used for housing.

We can therefore provide families with land as postulated by making a minor modification. Of the aggregate land surface, 5 percent will be used for housing. The additional 3 percent can be taken from agricultural land (2 percent) and land set aside for building (1 percent). Allowing for a population of 15 million, this would mean an average of 115 sq.m per person. Five persons (allowing for joint occupancy as below) would thus have 575 sq.m. The house and land and its surroundings could then be allocated as follows:

			sq.m
House and land	house		100
	miscellaneous:	parking	
		playing	
		flowerbeds, etc.	125
	food supply		300
	business purposes (optional)		50
			————
	total house and land		575
Services	shops		
	schools		
	social/cultural amenities		35
Greenery and traffic			90
			————
	TOTAL		700 sq.m

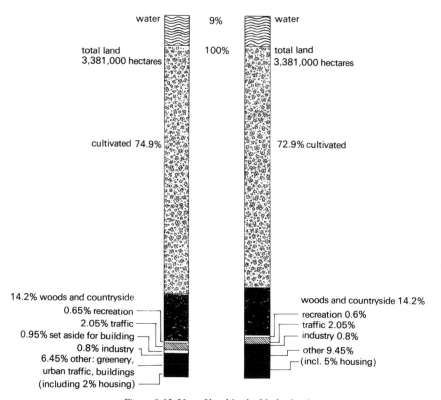

Figure 8.12 Use of land in the Netherlands

This means that, including services, a gross building density is obtained of 14.3 houses per hectare, (gross building density being defined as the number of houses per hectare of gross housing area; the gross housing area is the area for houses, gardens, and residential streets, including services, for 10,000 people). This can be compared with the building density figures in Table 8.3 (Ronteltap and Funken, 1972).

Table 8.3. Decrease in building density in the Netherlands

Old urban residential areas	150 or more houses/hectare
Urban expansion since 1945	70-40 houses/hectare
Ditto: smaller towns	40-20 houses/hectare
Current projects	30-20 houses/hectare
Planned projects	20 or fewer houses/hectare
For comparison:	
American expansion 1960-1970	10 houses/hectare

Home-job integration:

Wherever possible the job should be integrated with the home. Hence the design must allow for the addition of an office or workshop. This would close the functional gap between home and job which has helped to cause alienation from the family and society. It will also greatly reduce the need for transport.

The office or workshop is not located in the house because the space required will vary very greatly, while inconvenience must be avoided and it must be possible to extend the accommodation if required. The material and energy consumption for the office or workshop are not limited by the specification.

Adaptability:
A certain degree of adaptability will have to be guaranteed inside the house.

The house will have to be able to accommodate parents or invalid relatives or married children staying at home for the time being. It must be possible for all concerned to have some privacy. There will be more common family activities than at present and a comparatively large space must be allowed for these.

8.3.3 Design and comments

Bearing in mind the basic principles, the choice was a detached house. Its shape was determined largely by the need to limit heat losses. The various considerations led to a *pyramid shape*, in which the four sides running to an apex provide a relatively large amount of useful living space. Continuing the roof downwards below the upper-storey floor reduces the outside wall surface, which in this case provides much less insulation than the roof. The shape more or less corresponds to a traditional West Friesian farmhouse.

The glazed area has to be limited because heat losses through glass are much higher than with most other wall structures. Moreover, insulating of glazed structures is expensive and is comparatively ineffective. In order to obtain as much light as possible, however, glazing is largely fitted at an angle of 45°.

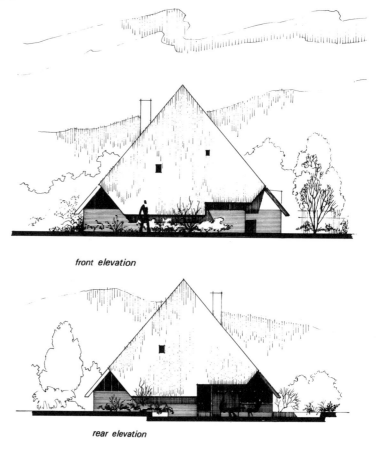

front elevation

rear elevation

Figure 8.13. Pyramid 2020 (front and rear)

Layout

Areas needing less heat act as buffer zones wherever possible. The main living accommodation consists of a central communication area with rooms around it for common pursuits such as dining, playing, hobbies, and music. Adjoining these are the patio and utilities: kitchen, storage/pantry, hall, and lavatory. The net ground-floor area is 104 sq.m. Bedrooms and bathroom are on the upper storey which has an area of 80 sq.m, half of it of walking height.

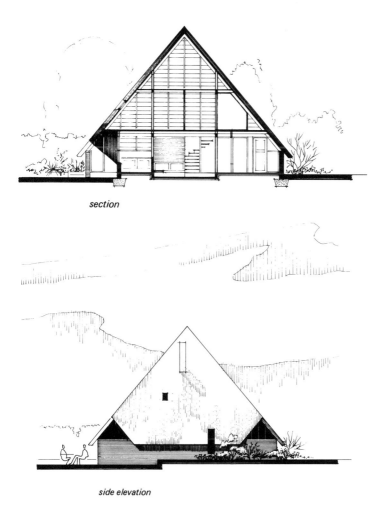

section

side elevation

Figure 8.14. Pyramid 2020 (section and side elevation)

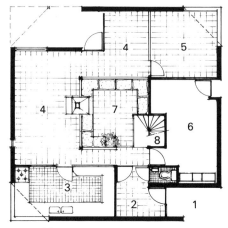

ground floor

Key:
1 entrance
2 hall, cloakroom, lavatory
3 kitchen
4 dining, playing
5 hobbies, music
6 storage, pantry
7 communication
8 staircase

9 hall
10 bathroom
11 bedroom

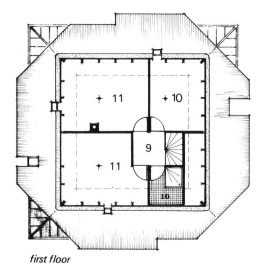

first floor

Figure 8.15. Pyramid 2020 (plan and first floor)

Materials

The choice of materials was guided by the following criteria:
- they must be made by low-energy processes causing little pollution;
- the materials used for outside surfaces must be good heat insulators;
- the use of natural materials should be encouraged for their psychological value;
- home-produced materials should be used wherever possible.

On this basis, the following materials were used:
- wood: upper-storey floor, roof structure, dividing walls, window and door frames and doors;
- brick: outside cavity walls (with mineral wool insulation);
- thatch: roof covering with fire protection on inside;
- poured concrete: ground floor and foundation strips (floor insulated with mineral-wool sheets).

Land

The land round the house could be divided up as shown in Figure 8.16.

Number of occupants

The house is intended for four to six persons. The estimates are based on an average of five.

Heat transmission

The heat-transmission calculations are based on heating for seven months of the year (5,100 hours) and an average outdoor temperature of 6°C, with indoor temperatures of:

living-room	20° C
hobbies and kitchen	18° C
storage	16° C
bedrooms	14° C
hall	12° C

The total heat loss is 8 million kcal. With a heating-installation efficiency of 60 percent the annual energy requirement is 13.3 million kcal., corresponding to 1,765 cu.m natural gas. For comparison, consumption by the average

Dutch home in 1975 was about 5,000 cu.m. It is therefore possible to build detached houses in the year 2020 which comply with our limits on the consumption of energy for space heating ($21.3 \times 10^6 - 42.6 \times 10^6$ kcal per annum for five occupants).

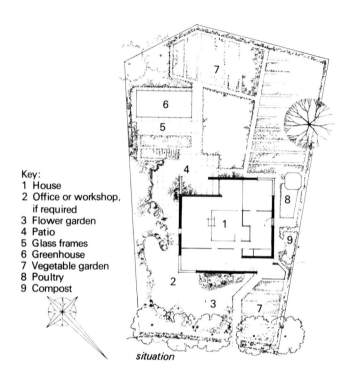

Key:
1 House
2 Office or workshop, if required
3 Flower garden
4 Patio
5 Glass frames
6 Greenhouse
7 Vegetable garden
8 Poultry
9 Compost

situation

Figure 8.16. Pyramid 2020 (layout of land)

Estimates

The complete estimates are given in Appendix C. Table 8.4 is a summary.

Table 8.4. Estimates for pyramid 2020

Item	Labour:		Materials	Energy
	man-hours	wages	($)	(kg CE)
Site work	57	286.67		
Concreting	228.3	1,148.33	281.11	860
Masonry	196.8	990.00	367.50	3,585
Tiling	10.4	52.50	16.67	35
Insulation	47.8	240.56	160.82	135
Carpentry	465.3	2,341.11	1,114.73	15
Roofing	270	1,358.06	1,000.00	
Glazing and painting	80.1	402.78	153.33	357
Steel and ironwork			235.56	151
Total	1,355.7	6,820.00	3,329.72	5,084

Conclusions

This house is quite practical for lower income groups in the year 2020. The use of steel is reduced to a minimum and is well within the limits. Energy consumption is very low indeed (20 percent of the permitted amount) because of the traditional building method and selective choice of materials. Energy consumption for space heating also remains within the limits.

9. Conclusions and evaluation

In recent years the United Nations and other organisations have repeatedly made recommendations:
- for limiting population growth and sharing prosperity among the entire world population;
- for limiting pollution of the environment and using natural resources responsibly.

This study, *Inhabiting the Earth as a Finite World* has tried to demonstrate how these recommendations might work out in practice. The income is indicated to which everyone would be entitled if prosperity were equitably shared, together with the quantities of materials and energy that could be used without exceeding specific limits.

A world simulation model defines the principal relationships between population, income, prosperity sharing, consumption of natural resources, pollution, food supplies, and housing.

Up to the year 2020 the population is expected to increase to 7 billion. Greater prosperity in the poor countries might lead to a reduction in the birth rate, so that a certain degree of stabilisation can gradually be reached. Let us hope it will be possible to feed this vast number of people.

As regards the sharing of prosperity between rich and poor nations, the ultimate aim is equality of incomes. The average income in the rich countries is likely to go on growing, but only by 1 to 2 percent per annum until the year 2000, after which it will become stabilised. Nevertheless, the wealthiest of all (5 percent of the world population) will see their incomes drop by 20 percent.

An increase in development aid will make it possible for the poor nations' per capita income to increase considerably. This income will grow by an average of 5.2 percent per annum and in fifty years' time will be over twelve times as high. By the year 2020 a man in a rich country will still be earning one and a half times as much as a man in a poor country. Development aid is not only a matter of sending money, but – of greater importance – the transfer of expertise and technology to enable the poor nations to initiate their own self-sustained development. Experience in the rich nations has shown that advancing prosperity had deleterious side-effects, including pollution, cardio-vascular diseases, individual isolation, aggressiveness, urbanisation, a high road-accident death rate, etc. It is to be hoped that the poor nations can organise their societies so as to avoid these disastrous attributes of prosperity.

The study devotes special attention to building materials. The annual consumption of natural resources is limited to 1 percent of the current year's reserves. There is an almost total lack of some materials, such as copper, lead, zinc, and aluminium; their use will have to be kept to a minimum, with very strict limits on steel consumption. For instance, only enough is allowed for a self-supported concrete floor of 50 sq.m and some essential ironwork. This obviously imposes limitations on wide spans, frameworks, and even columns. By contrast, supplies of timber are ample. Together with the latest methods of wood preserving (and fireproofing) and conversion (especially bonding methods) this may lead to a revaluation of this traditional material. The use of plastics compares well with other building materials, both from the point of view of energy requirements and durability and ecological harmlessness. Perhaps they could become alternatives to steel?

Another striking thing is that fossil fuel reserves are still enormous. A presumed shortage of energy is not, therefore, an adequate argument for the large-scale use of nuclear power. Nevertheless, we have reduced energy consumption as much as possible because of the high cost and the adverse effects on the environment.

The limitations on the consumption of natural resources and energy and on pollution will undoubtedly require comprehensive supervision of all production processes; this must not, of course, result in excessive planning and controls. A large measure of autonomy is still conceivable in separate regions to allow for local opportunities and needs. The exchange of surpluses would also help to prevent the system becoming too rigid.

In order to give a clear sketch of the possibilities under the new conditions, we have endeavoured to design houses that can be built within the limits for materials, energy, and cost. They show that people can *live in this world and not at the expense of the world.* In envisaging future possibilities, we shall at all times have to realise that we are concerned with the needs and reactions of man as he was but in new conditions.

While the designs were being made, the extent to which thinking is based unconsciously on industrial production, the large-scale approach, standardisation, and prefabrication became clearer and clearer. The presentation of new data, such as limiting the consumption of natural resources, saving energy, and safeguarding the environment, however, were bound to lead to a different approach. There had to be a change-over to simple, carefully devised methods and very selective use of materials. In keeping with the fineness of ecological processes, building methods can develop best on the basis of producing smal groups of houses. Manual production methods can blow new life into the arts and crafts.

The projects are a more or less arbitrary choice of different types of houses. In conurbations there will have to be identifiable groups of housing units. Within the scope of our study the aspects of complete settlements could only be dealt with incidentally. One of the projects showed the possibility of harmonising the functions of the home and the job, services and nature.

Although our research was based on stabilisation of the population, limitation of material and energy consumption, protection of the environment, and the sharing of prosperity, the result is not a completely static society. Though exponential growth must be stopped, there are adequate prospects for the future, such as the development of clean energy sources, alternative materials, recycling methods, and more durable consumer goods.

It has been reiterated in this study that even a scientific approach is not faultless. An ample margin of error must be allowed for in all the figures and ratios. We do not claim to be putting forward either the only solution or the only proper solution. But we do believe it would be worth trying out one or more of the designs to prove their feasibility. Moreover, there is a pressing need for similarly detailed analyses on subjects other than housing.

We are very pleased to add that there is now considerable interest in building the pyramid 2020 in the Netherlands.

Appendix A: Some major air pollutants

Pollutant	Sources	Quantity	Distribution in environment	Estimated level	Relevant interactions	Effects on health	Effects on environment	Notes
Carbon dioxide (CO_2)	Use of carboniferous fuels for producing energy, for heating and transport.	1.5×10^{10} tonne/year	World-wide	Normally 320 ppm.	Biological processes form a natural system for assimilation and replenishment of CO_2.	Indirectly only, by possible changes in world climate.	Possible increase in temperature of earth's surface (long-term).	Normal constituent of the atmosphere; essential for plant life.
Carbon monoxide (CO)	Incomplete combustion of carbon-containing matter (automobiles, industrial processes, solid waste disposal, forest fires).	2.5×10^8 tonne/year	Local and regional	Depends very much on local conditions; maximum near heavy traffic: 20 – 120 ppm; average in cities: 1 – 10 ppm.	CO oxidises rather slowly in the lower atmosphere; it is chemically inactive and hardly reacts with other constituents.	Through attachment of CO to haemoglobin in the red blood corpuscles, the transport of oxygen through the body is impeded; poisoning causes in first instance poorer brain function and ultimately death.	No effects on higher plant life at concentrations under 100 ppm for one to three weeks.	There are various natural sources, but their share in the world level is considered slight; small amounts are produced in man and other animals.
Sulphur dioxide (SO_2)	Energy and heat production from sulphur-containing fossil fuels; industrial processes (sulphuric acid factories).	1.5×10^8 tonne/year	Local and regional	Annual average in polluted conurbations: 0.1 – 0.15 ppm.	(a) atmospheric oxidation to SO_2 leads to formation of sulphuric acid haze and sulphates; (b) absorption and chemical reactions with suspended particulate matter.	In combination with air particles (smoke) aggravates existing respiratory disorders and encourages their development.	(a) chronic damage to vegetation at 0.03 ppm; sensitive varieties are affected at 0.3 ppm for 8 hours; sulphuric acid haze causes leaf damage at 0.1 mg/cu.m; (b) affects visibility (sulphuric acid haze and sulphates); (c) attacks materials, increases corrosion (mainly by sulphuric acid); (d) acidifies soil and water.	Natural sources such as volcanic gases cause about 20% of the total.

Pollutant	Sources	Quantity	Distribution in environment	Estimated level	Relevant interactions	Effects on health	Effects on environment	Notes
Nitrogen oxides (NO/NO_2)	High-temperature combustion is attended by oxidation of atmospheric nitrogen; industrial processes (sulphuric acid and nitric acid manufacture); forest fires.	5.3×10^7 tonne/year	Local and regional	Usually less than 0.1 ppm; 1 ppm where traffic is frequent.	NO is converted in the astmosphere into NO_2, partly under the influence of sunlight; photochemical oxidation of NO in the presence of hydrocarbons makes the aire irritating (ozone).	Possible increase in acute respiratory infections and death of newly born children from bronchitis.	(a) brown mist in urban air; (b) level at which vegetation is harmed is above normal atmospheric level; local effects on woods near industrial sites.	
Hydrocarbon (C_xH_y)	Partial combustion of carbon-containing fuel (automobiles); industrial processes; solid waste disposal; solvents; forest fires.		Local and regional	In badly polluted regions maximum hourly level up to 10 ppm (measured as carbon).	Reacting constituents play an important role in forming the oxidising forms of pollution.	Most effects are caused by atmospheric reactions; some oxidation products irritate the eyes (aldehydes).	(a) some compounds, such as ethylene, are highly toxic; sensitive plants are damaged at 0.005 ppm; (b) poorer visibility due to small particles, mainly owing to atmospheric reactions; (c) unpleasant smell.	This group comprises the atmospheric hydrocarbons (mainly CH_4).
Dust/smoke	Fuel combustion; industrial processes (cement industry, oxy-steel processing, iron foundries); solid waste incineration; burning waste on farms and in forestry.	2×10^7 tonne/year	Local, regional, world-wide	Annual urban average: 40 – 400 μg/cu.m.	A very varied group of chemicals; mostly occurring in groups owing to their physical behaviour.	Possibility of poisoning depending on chemical composition (including lead and asbestos); dust finer than 5 microns penetrates into innermost	(a) increasing cloud and fog; limitation of direct sunlight and visibility; (b) damage to materials and contamination; (c) possible long-term effect on	Natural sources are dust clouds and deserts, volcanic eruptions, sea mist (sea salt); stratospheric particles are mainly of natural origin.

Pollutant	Sources	Quantity	Distribution in environment	Estimated level	Relevant interactions	Effects on health	Effects on environment	Notes
						bronchial tube where lead and cadmium especially have very harmful effects; effects in combination with gaseous pollutants such as SO_2 are greater than the sum-total of the individual effects.	temperature of earth's surface.	
Fluorides	Industrial processes (steel and aluminium production, brickworks, glass factories, superphosphate factories); coal combustion, waste incineration.		Local	Average concentration in various American cities 0.001 – 0.02 ppm.	Fluride ions inhibit some enzymes.	Low concentrations in drinking water reduce risk of dental caries (1 mg/l); teeth are stained at higher concentrations (2-8 mg daily); at still higher concentrations possible damage to bone structure.	(a) fluorosis in grazing animals; (b) damage to vegetation at concentrations of 0.002 ppm; (c) metal corrosion; damage to many building materials.	

Source: Melgert and Mok (1973).

Appendix B: Technical life of the house

Method I

This method, worked out by the Central Bureau of Statistics, is given in *Statistische en econometrische onderzoekingen*, Volume 9, 1st Quarter 1954. The calculations are based on the number of housing units at the end of 1970, and the age structure for these units was recorded. In the case of post-1920 houses, this involves no problems because detailed figures are available. For the period before this, only estimates exist (Duyndam, 1941). Table B.1 gives the age structure of existing houses and the gross increase by ten-year periods.

The difference between the two columns is due to an adjustment of 76,000 units prematurely destroyed through the war. The average technical life can be found from Table B.2 by cumulation of the gross increase.

The cumulative total is compared with the number of units on 31 December, 1970 (3,787,000). By adding houses built from 1860 to 1869, the 1970 end-of-year stock is exceeded by 11,000. This is about 10% of the houses built during

Table B.1

Year	Number (thousands)	Gross increase (thousands)
1961-70	1,075	1,075
1951-60	734	734
1941-50	214	214
1931-40	414	430
1921-30	455	472
1910-20	177	184
1900-09	189	196
1890-99	164	170
1880-89	125	130
1870-79	135	140
1860-69	105	120
1850-59		100

Table B.2

Year	Increase (thousands) (incl. adjustments for wartime)	Cumulation (thousands)
1961-70	1,075	1,075
1951-60	734	1,809
1941-50	214	2,023
1931-40	414	2,437
1921-30	455	2,892
1910-20	177	3,069
1900-09	189	3,258
1890-99	164	3,422
1880-89	125	3,547
1870-79	135	3,682
1860-69	116	3,798

this period. The oldest house at 31 December, 1970 thus dates from 1861. The average technical life is therefore equal to the period from 1 January, 1861 to 31 December, 1970, or 110 years.

Method II

This method was taken from L. Tas (1969). The mortality rate for a given age group of houses is the quotient of the number of withdrawals and the stock of units at the beginning of the period. For a number of years, figures are available for the ages of the units withdrawn from stock. By reference to these, the mortality rate for a given age group can be calculated. The results are given in Table B.1.

Table B.1

Age group	Mortality rate per 100,000 units
Before 1801	611
1801-1850	2,148
1851-1875	1,770
1876-1900	1,491
1901-1925	433
1926-1950	178
1951-or later	18

The figures are shown as a graph in Figure B.2.

The curve is accurate enough as a basis for a broad estimate. The survival chances and mortality rates for ten-year groups can be tabulated from the graph (see Table B.4).

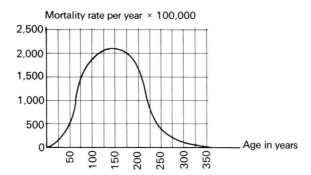

Figure B.2. Mortality rate of houses

Houses older than 250 years (4.2 percent of those in 1970) are assumed to reach an average of 300 years. The average technical life is now found to be 108 years. This computation assumes that past mortality rates have remained unchanged. But if action is taken in the future to stop houses degenerating into slums, the normative life would be 85 years. As an illustration, the survival chances in both calculations are given in Figure B.3.

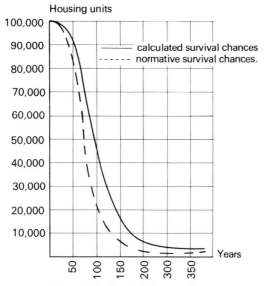

Figure B.3. Survival chance of houses

Table B.4

Age group	Survival chance (beginning of period)	Mortality rate per age group
0 - 9 years	1.000	0.002
10 - 19 years	0.998	7
20 - 29 years	991	16
30 - 39 years	976	27
40 - 49 years	950	39
50 - 59 years	0.912	0.066
60 - 69 years	852	111
70 - 79 years	757	142
80 - 89 years	649	157
90 - 99 years	547	168
100 - 109 years	0.456	0.176
110 - 119 years	375	183
120 - 129 years	306	187
130 - 139 years	249	189
140 - 149 years	202	189
150 - 159 years	0.164	0.187
160 - 169 years	133	183
170 - 179 years	109	175
180 - 189 years	90	166
190 - 199 years	75	152
200 - 209 years	0.064	0.130
210 - 219 years	55	98
220 - 229 years	50	69
230 - 239 years	46	51
240 - 249 years	44	37

Appendix C:
Detailed estimates for pyramid 2020

Item	Unit	Quantity	Man-hours per unit	Price per unit ($)	Energy per unit	Man-hours total	Wages total ($)	Material total ($)	Energy total (kg CE)	Notes
Site work										
Removing turves (10 cm top surface) + storage	m^2	150	0.3			30	150.83			
Removing topsoil + spreading over ave. 10 m run	m^3	19.3	1.4			27	135.83			
TOTAL SITE WORK						57	286.66			
Concreting										
Poured concrete footings:	m^3	14.6	6	8.60		87.6	440.56	125.56		ratio 1:4:8
Cement	kg	2,190			0.17				372	150 kg cem/m^3
Sand	kg	11,096			0.001				11	0.475 m^3 sand/m^3
Gravel	kg	21,080			0.001				21	0.95 m^3 gravel/m^3
Formwork	m^2	4	1.1	2.78		4.4	22.22	11.11		
Poured concrete ground floor:	m^3	11	6	8.60		66	331.91	94.72		
Cement	kg	1,650			0.17				280	
Sand	kg	8,350			0.001				8	
Gravel	kg	17,765			0.001				17	
Stabilised sand	m^3	5.4	0.5	5.28	15.7	2.7	13.61	28.33	85	
Finishing floor (cem./sand)	m^2	104	0.65	7.96		67.6	340.00	16.67		
Cement	kg	693			0.17				106	
Sand	kg	2,940			0.001				3	
Petrol	l	20		0.24	0.001			4.72	10	
TOTAL CONCRETING						228.3	1,148.30	281.11	913	
Masonry										
Cavity wall (incl. pointing)	m^2	60	2.9		0.31	174	875.28		2,790	work-time includes: positioning, scaffolding, hod-carrying, mixing mortar 1:1:4 265 kn cem/m^3 0.211 m^3 lime/m^3 0.844 m^3 sand/m^3
Bricks	l	9,000		33.34				300.00	305	
Mortar	m^3	2.44		6.67	125.3			16.25		
Inside masonry	m^2	6	1.3			7.8	39.17			
Bricks	l	500		33.34				16.67	155	
Mortar	m^3	0.2		6.67				1.39	25	
Chimney	l	1,000		33.34	125	15	75.56	33.33	310	
TOTAL MASONRY						196.8	990.01	367.64	3,585	

Item	Unit	Quantity	Man-hours per unit	Price per unit ($)	Energy per unit	Man-hours total	Wages total ($)	Material total ($)	Energy total (kg CE)	Notes
Tiling										
Wall tiles	m²	2	2.5	2.63		5	25.28	5.28		amounts incl. mortar
Flooring tiles	m²	3	1.8	3.80		5.4	27.22	11.39	35	
TOTAL TILING						10.4	52.50	26.67	35	
Insulation										
Plastic foil	m²	104		0.17		3	15.00	17.33		
Mineral wool 5 cm thick	m²	104	0.2	0.88		20.8	104.72	91.00	135	
Cavity-wall insulation	m²	60	0.4	0.88		24	120.83	52.50		
TOTAL INSULATION						47.8	240.55	160.83	135	

Item	Unit	Quantity	Man-hours per unit	Price per unit ($)	Energy per unit	Man-hours total	Wages total ($)	Material total ($)	Energy total (kg CE)	Notes
Carpentry										
Outside window and door frames	m²	20,4	2			40.8	205.28	54.17		0.65 m³
Matchboard doors	1	2	2.5	5.56		5	25.28	11.11		0.14 m³
Garden door	1	1	2			2	10.00	2.78		0.037 m³
Positioning door and window frames						32	161.11			
Double panel (tongue and groove)	m²	3	1.5	4.17		4.5	22.78	12.50		0.15 m³
Wall plate 6 × 16 cm	m¹	42	0.27	0.68		11.3	56.94	28.61		0.40 m³
Columns 16 × 16 cm	m¹	23		1.81		6	30.28	41.67		0.67 m³
Bridging beams 6 × 16 cm	m¹	22	0.27	0.68		6	30.28	15.00		0.20 m³
Corner posts 6 × 16 cm	m¹	42	0.26	0.68		10.9	54.72	28.61		0.40 m³
Rafters 5 × 10 cm	m¹	210		0.42		30	150.83	87.50		1.10 m³
Laths 3 × 6 cm	m¹	630	0.028	0.17		18	90.56	105.00		1.20 m³
Attic beams 5 × 15 cm	m¹	27	0.2	0.50		5.4	27.22	13.61		0.20 m³
Tongue and groove, 1.4 cm thick	m²	25	0.4	1.74		10	50.28	43.33		0.294 m³
Second-storey floor, 21 mm thick	m²	83	0.4	1.74		33.2	166.94	144.44		1.75 m³
Bearers 8 × 18 cm	m¹	40		0.90		12	60.28	36.11		0.38 m³
Boarding joists 5 × 15 cm	m¹	90		0.51		20	100.56	45.56		0.68 m³
Compressed-reed beams	m²	83	0.25	1.00		21.75	109.72	83.05		
Scarf strips 2 × 2 cm	m¹	225		0.04				9.44		0.10 m³
Lining 5 × 7 cm	m¹	210	0.25	0.26		52.5	264.17	53.61		0.74 m³
Tongue and groove 1.4 cm thick, ground floor	m²	42	0.5	1.74		21	105.56	73.06		0.59 m³
Ditto, first floor	m²	78	0.5	1.74		39	196.11	135.83		1.09 m³
Liners 5 × 7 cm (glazed front ground floor)	m¹	80	0.4	0.26		32	161.11	20.56		0.28 m³
Batten doors	1	6		0.16		3	15.00	15.83		0.14 m³
Glazed doors	1	3	2	2.78		6	30.28	8.33		0.11 m³
Cleats 2 × 15 cm	m¹	18		0.31				5.56		0.05 m³
Final hanging						12	60.28			
Open staircase	1	12	1			25	125.83	27.78		0.12 m³
Woodwork for refuse sorting bin						6	30.28	11.67		0.12 m³
TOTAL CARPENTRY						465.35	2,341.68	1,114.72	15	11.6 m³ timber
Roofing										
Thatched roof	m²	200	1.15	3.33		230	1,156.94	666.67		
Fire protection	m²	200	0.2	1.67		40	201.11	333.33		
TOTAL ROOFING						270	1,358.05	1,000.00		

Glazing and Painting									
Double glazing (normal thickness)	m²	12.5	1.15	3.11		18.8	94.44	38.89	
Linseed oil putty	kg	10		0.12				1.25	
Inside glazing (normal)	m²	26	0.75	1.56		19.5	98.05	40.56	
Wired glass (near terrace)	m²	4	0.75	3.89		3	15.00	15.56	
Total glazing	kg	510			0.7				357
Oiling door and window frames (3×)	m²	24	0.45			10.8	54.44	8.33	
Linseed oil	m²	5		1.67				8.33	
Oiling t. and g. (inside)	kg	140	0.2			28	140.83		
Oil	kg	30		1.67				50.00	
						80.1	402.76	154.59	357
TOTAL GLAZING AND PAINTING									
Steel and ironwork, furniture									
Ties for fixing thatch	kg	40		0.21	1			8.33	40
Braces 30 × 5 for floor beams	kg	16		0.21	1			3.33	16
Cavity ties	kg	8		0.21	1			1.67	8
Sundries (small ironwork)	kg	65		2.08	1			135.42	65
Hinges	kg	7		3.47	1			24.31	7
Locks, door handles	kg	15		4.17	1			62.50	15
TOTAL STEEL								235.56	151

Appendix D: Heat and sound insulation

Heat insulation

As energy becomes more expensive steps will obviously have to be taken to cut its consumption. Particularly in regions where major temperature fluctuations are common, good heat insulation is essential. It can be achieved with properly insulated structures.

The insulating capacity of a structure is expressed as the coefficient of heat transmission (k). It is built up of the thermal-conductivity coefficient and the heat-transfer coefficient. The thermal conductivity coefficient of all materials is known and is indicated by the symbol λ (lambda). The lower the value required for k, the better the insulation must be. Good insulation can be obtained by using highly insulating materials such as corkboards, polystyrene foam, or synthetic-fibre blankets. Corkboard or polystyrene sheet 2.5 cm thick, for instance, has the same insulating properties as a 36 cm brick wall or a concrete wall 120 cm thick. But this does not mean that a brick wall can simply be replaced by insulating board. Such boards have little accumulating capacity; rooms get warm quickly but cool quickly too, as in army barracks. It is thus better to combine a good insulating material of the requisite thickness with the traditional structure.

Table D.1 gives the values of k for some common structures.

Table D.1 Building structures and values of k

Outside wall structures	k
Half-brick masonry	2.8
Single-brick masonry	1.65
$1\frac{1}{2}$-brick masonry	1.4
Half-brick - cavity - half-brick (incl. plastering)	1.4
Half-brick - cavity $1\frac{1}{2}$ cm polystyrene foam - half-brick	0.9
Half-brick - cavity 2 cm polystyrene foam - half-brick	0.75
Half-brick - cavity 4 cm polystyrene foam - half-brick	0.5
Half-brick - cavity 6 cm polystyrene foam - half-brick	0.375
Half-brick - cavity - 18 cm concrete	1.5

Half-brick - cavity 1½ cm polystyrene foam - 18 cm concrete	0.95
Concrete 10 cm	3.7
Concrete 18 cm	3.0
Hollow-brick elements of 20 cm-thick lightweight concrete	1.4
Glass per sq.m, 4 mm thick	5
Glass per sq.m, 10 mm thick	5
Double glazing, 12 mm air cavity	2.7
Triple glazing	1.8
Double-glazed windows (movable)	3.1
Outside door unglazed	3
Outside door glazed	4
Sandwich panels of:	
Metal sheet - 4 cm polystyrene foam - metal sheet	0.6
Asbestos cement sheet - 4 cm polystyrene foam - board	0.56
Asbestos cement sheet - 4 cm cork - board	0.58

Roofing structures

Flat roof consisting of:	
2 layers roofing felt - 18 mm wooden parts	2
2 layers roofing felt - 18 mm wooden parts - 17 cm air cavity - plastering	1.4
Ditto with softboard	1.3
2 layers roofing felt - 30 mm insulated roofing sheet	0.9
Ditto 40 mm	0.7
2 layers roofing felt - lightweight concrete 8.5 cm thick - 2 cm polystyrene foam	0.93
2 layers roofing felt - lightweight concrete 17 cm thick - 2 cm polystyrene foam	0.7
Roofing tiles - 18 mm roof boarding	2.7
Ditto finished with hardboard	1.5
Roofing tiles - roofing sheet insulated with 2 cm-thick polyurethane foam	1

Floor structures

Wooden floor, parts 22 mm	2.5
Ditto - 4 cm mineral wool sheets	0.6
Lightweight concrete prefabricated flooring	1.5
Ditto - 4 cm mineral wool sheets	0.5

Sound insulation

Sound insulation is another matter requiring attention in the houses of the future. An occupant of a terraced house the load-bearing walls of which are too light, will be troubled by noise from his neighbours. The structure should be built so that noise transmitted from one house to another is kept to a minimum. The same applies to the interior of the house.

On the whole, there are two distinct forms of noise transmission: contact and airborne. Contact noise may be caused by walking on a floor or staircase, drilling or hammering. Airborne noise comes from talking, singing, music. Different measures in building are required to stop the two forms becoming a nuisance. They aim at reducing the side-effects to levels at which inconvenience is avoided. A good example of stopping contact and airborne noise is a cavity wall between two houses. If optimum benefit is to be derived from this, additional measures are required as regards footings, outside walls, and roof structure.

Sound is usually expressed as decibels (dB). Zero is the limit of audibility, while 140 dB is the threshold of pain. Table D.2 lists the strength of a number of sources.

The insulating value of a structure can be expressed in dB. The more robust a wall, window pane, or ceiling, the better its sound insulation. A $1\frac{1}{2}$-brick wall, for instance, gives 50 dB insulation. From one house to the next, the sound of a radio set with a volume of 65 dB is then reduced to 15 dB. Figure D.1 gives the sound insulation levels of a number of structures.

Table D.2 Sound levels of various sources

Source	dB
Limit of audibility	0
Rustling leaves	20
Reading room	30
Quiet music	40
Office	50
Conversation	60
Department store	65
Traffic artery	70/80
Loud radio set	80
Printing works, engine room	90
Car hooter (close to)	100
Pneumatic hammer (close to)	110
Machine gun	120
50 metres from jet plane taking off	130
Threshold of pain	140

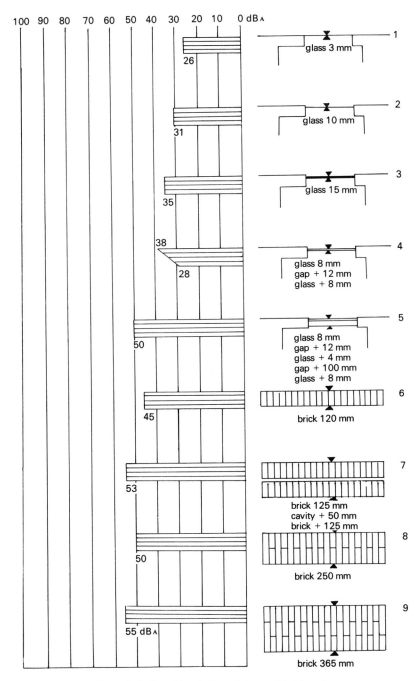

Figure D.1. Sound insulation of glass and brickwork

Bibliography

Abrams, Ch., 1964, *Housing in the modern world*, London.

Alexander, C., 1964, *Notes on the synthesis of form*, Cambridge Mass.

Apostel, L., 1960, Towards the formal study of models in the non-formal sciences, in: *Synthèse*, 12.

Arendt, H., 1959, *The human condition*, New York.

Beer, St., 1966, *Decision and control*, London.

Bertels, K. and Nauta, D., 1969, *Inleiding tot het modelbegrip*, Bussum.

'Blueprint for survival' (Blauwdruk voor Overleving), *Maandblad voor Milieudefensie*, jg. 1, nrs. 1 en 2.

Bogue, D. J., 1969, *Principles of demography*, New York.

Bol, W., 1974, *Hout als energiebron*, Eindhoven.

Bouwcentrum, 1970a, *Elementenbegroting*, Rotterdam.

Bouwcentrum, 1970b, *Richtprijzen van bouwmaterialen*, Rotterdam.

Bouwcentrum, 1972, *International course on house building costs in West-Africa*, Rotterdam.

van Bremen, H., 1974, 'Energieverbruik voor bouwen en wonen,' in: *Bouw*, nr. 21.

Browning, B. L., 1963, *The chemistry of wood*, New York.

Buckley, W., 1967, *Sociology and modern systems theory*, Englewood Cliffs, New Jersey.

Buringh, P., van Heemst, H. D. J., Staring, G. J., 1975, *Computation of the absolute maximum food production of the world*, Wageningen.

Carson, R., 1963, *Silent spring*, New York.

Central Bureau of Statistics, 1954, 'Balanswaarde van en afschrijvingen op woningen,' in: *Statistische en Econometrische Onderzoekingen*, Vol. 9.

Central Bureau of Statistics, 1973, *Pocket Yearbook*, 's-Gravenhage.

Central Planning Bureau, 1975, *Economische gevolgen van bestrijding van milieuverontreiniging*, 's-Gravenhage.

Commoner, B., 1971, 'Economic growth and ecology, a sociologist's view,' in: *Monthly Labour Review*.

Duyndam, J. A. G. M., 1941, 'De ontwikkeling van de woningvoorraad in Nederland sinds omstreeks 1800, de noodzakelijke vernieuwing van de woningvoorraad en de toekomstige woningproduktie,' in: *Tijdschrift voor Volkshuisvesting en Stedebouw*.

Van Ettinger, J., 1969, 'Wereldvolkshuisvestingsvraagstukken', in: *Bouw*, nr. 7.

Fao, 1971, *Yearbook of forest products 1960-1970*, Rome.

Foqué, R., 1975, *Ontwerpsystemen, een inleiding tot de ontwerptheorie*, Utrecht.

Foqué, R., 1976, 'Beyond design methods, arguments on a practical design theory,' 1st European Design Research Conference, invited paper, Portsmouth.

Hubbert, M. K., 1968, *Energy resources, National Academy of Sciences*, National Research Council, Publ. 1000-D.

Illich, I., 1973, 'Energie, vitesse et justice sociale,' in: *Le Monde*, June 5.

Illich, I., 1973b, *Energieverbruik en maatschappelijke tegenstellingen*, Baarn.

Interimnota inkomensbeleid, 1975, Staatsuitgeverij, 's-Gravenhage.

Jelsma, O., 1973, *Begrotingen uit de bouwwereld*, Rotterdam.

Jones, J. C., 1970, *Design methods, seeds of human futures*, London.

Kloos, P., 1972, 'Caraïbendorp in Suriname,' in: *Forum*, Vol. 23, nr. 3.

Kreyger, P. C., 1974, *Environment, pollution, energy and materials*, Eindhoven.

Lesuis, P. J. J. and Muller, F., 1976, 'Perspectives on short term energy shortages in the Netherlands,' in: M. Chatterji, P. van Rompuy (ed.), *Energy, regional science and public policy. Lecture notes in economics and mathematical systems*, Berlin.

Linneman, H., 1976, *Food for a growing world population*, Amsterdam.

Van der Maarel, E., 1971, 'Florastatistiek als bijdrage tot de evaluatie van natuurgebieden,' in: *Gorteria* 5, nr. 7/10.

McLuhan, T. C., 1973, *Want de aarde is onze moeder*, Baarn.

Maturana, H., McCulloch, W. and Pitts, W., 1959, 'What the frog's eye tells to the frog's brain, in: *Proc. Ire* 47.

Meadows, D. L., 1972, *The limits to growth*, New York (Report of the Club of Rome, Utrecht, 1972).

Meadows, W. L., Behrens, W. W. et al, 1974, *Dynamics of growth in a finite world*, Cambridge Mass.

Van der Meiden, H. A., 1971, 'Nieuwe bossen in Nederland,' in: *Nederlands Bosbouw Tijdschrift*.

Melgert, W. J. and Mok, Ph. G., 1973, *Het relaas van het begin*, De Stockholm Conferentie over het leefmilieu, Amsterdam.

Mesarovic, M. and Pestel, E., 1974, *Mankind at the turning point*, Amsterdam.

Ministry of Foreign Affairs, 1974, *Het Nederlandse ontwikkelingsgebied*, 's-Gravenhage.

Misset's Bouwwereld, 1970, jaargang 66, nr. 1 (Richtprijzen van bouwmaterialen).

Muller, F., and Pelupessy, W., 1971, 'Economische waardering van de schaarse lucht in Rijnmond,' in: *ESB*, 31 maart 1971.

Muller, F., 1972, 'Socio-economic policy in the Club of Rome's world model,' Erasmus University Rotterdam, Discussion Paper Series, nr. 7501/6.

Muller, F., Trapman, J. and Foqué, R., 1976, *Inhabiting a finite but equitable world*, 's-Gravenhage.

Muller, F., 1978, *Energy and environment in interregional input-output models*, Martinus Nijhoff, Leiden/Boston.

Peters, H., 1973, *De wet van behoud van ellende*, Amsterdam.

Platt, J., 1969, 'What must we do?' in: *Science*.

Rakhlin, I. V. and Koshkin, L. I., 1972, in: *Soviet Plastics*, nr. 1.

Ronteltap, R. and Funken, J. 1972, *Ruimteconsumptie of bouwconsumptie; sociale kosten van de wijze van wonen en verplaatsen*, Deventer.

Sauvy, A., 1973, *Croissance Zéro*, Paris.

Schuur, G., 1973, 'Milieu, grondstoffen en kunststoffen,' in: *Plastica*, vol. 26.

Tas, L., 1969, 'Sterftecijfers voor woningen,' in: *Bouw*, nr. 13.

Tinbergen, J., 1975, *Income distribution, analysis and policies*, Amsterdam.

Tinbergen, J., 1976, *Naar een rechtvaardiger internale orde* (Reshaping the International Order), Amsterdam/Brussel.

Ward, B. and Dubos, R., 1972, *Only one Earth; the care and maintenance of a small planet*, New York.

Wieser, W., 1959, *Organismen, Strukturen, Maschinen*, Frankfurt a.M.

World Power Conference, 1968, *Survey of energy resources*, London.

Index